What Others Are Saying about the Quest Effect:

"Real learning occurs when you find a traditional framework applied in a new, deep, and exciting way. *The Quest Effect* meets this challenge. This book makes the process of authentic transformation accessible. It is well written, based on proven results, and offers a unique depth of insight. It offers a language that, in itself, makes it a great book."

—Peter Block, bestselling author and consultant

"*The Quest Effect* may be the first book devoted to the corporate quest. It taps ancient wisdom and also new science to reveal the big idea behind breakthrough change. The book is practical and accessible—the result of the author's deep experience consulting to organizations. It is also a leap of imagination that draws on intersections of knowledge outside the traditional business realm. This fascinating book will challenge many stereotypes of organizational transformation."

—Bernard Booms, Professor Emeritus,
University of Washington School of Business

"Randall Benson presents a business model for reinstating the spirit of entrepreneurial leadership in organizations. The Quest process facilitates a 'values shift' within the organization, a willingness to consider breakthrough change as a means to sustain the 'prime' phase of the corporate lifecycle. He addresses the conditions that can stifle change initiatives and he nurtures a passionate commitment to higher vision and openness to discovery."

—Stephanie Galindo, Student Dean, The Adizes Graduate Institute

W9-AUO-040

This book is for anyone that wants to move from focusing on "why we can't make positive change" to the adventure of "what will it take to get there?" The author's wisdom, gained from a career of transforming organizations, provides every reader with that "special something" that it takes for us all to achieve the "unachievable".

— *Joan Wellman, President, Joan Wellman and Associates, Inc.*

"I think every organization in America should be using the Quest approach."

—*Rob Anderson, COO, Equitable Life & Casualty*

"[The Quest Effect] becomes far more than just a map of the journey but a tool to guide the way."

—*Gayle Young, Associate Editor, The Integral Leadership Review.*

Dedicated to my mentor and steadfast friend, Bernard Booms, who encouraged me at every step of my journey.

— *Randall Benson*

Acknowledgements

Several generous people provided essential support to me during my writing odyssey. I would like to acknowledge them here. Bernard Booms encouraged me from the conception of the book theme to its publication. Margaret Smith did a magical job creating readable language out of my early drafts. Bob Wiebe provided me with critical insights on the nature of breakthrough. Gayle Young shared her poetic inflection and personal wisdom of the quest. Kim Dodson was a brilliant thought partner who helped me sort out difficult concepts. Gill Sandy helped me find my own mission in the writing of this book. My wife, Stella, gave up many evenings with me so I could create the book. I offer my heartfelt gratitude to all of them.

The Quester may start with a formless hunch; a powerful yet shadowy intuition that indicates the basic shape, the source from which the quest is calling him. The form will appear out of the adventures, the trials, and the learning. This is why a constantly changing process is not a process of confusion but one of growth.

— Parabola

Contents

Phase Four: Renewal

Why Quest?

A human being is born to set out on this quest, his quest, like a knight of Arthur's court.
> —Dorothea Matthews Dooling, *in* The Spirit of Quest

What makes us really human? Philosophers and scientists have long argued about it. I believe it is our innate propensity to quest.
> — Charles Pasternak, *biochemist, author of* The Quest

For more than twenty years, I have been involved in organizational transformations and the breakthroughs that drive them. I have discovered that successful transformations characteristically possess an unexplained element, and that is the principle of quest. The quest often means the difference between stalled efforts and extraordinary transformations.

This was a difficult conclusion for me to embrace. I began my management consulting work on the process side of transformations: the Toyota Production System, Six Sigma Quality, Service System Design, and other process work. I worked exclusively in the field of process transformation. I helped my clients master the tools of process and adopting process methods that were radical at the time.

As time went on, though, I felt more and more uneasy about the true drivers of breakthrough and transformation. Why were the most effective implementers of new methods not always the most effective at moving to new levels of performance? Why didn't those who followed our change programs achieve great results every time?

To answer these questions, I considered several popular adages:
- The culture wasn't empowering.
- Top leadership wasn't committed.
- We hadn't reached a critical mass with our training.
- The client didn't perfectly fit the profile for the methodology.
- We failed to communicate sufficiently.
- Too much change was happening too fast.
- We didn't place enough emphasis on change management.

But these notions failed to satisfy, because organizations most successful at transformation had made plenty of mistakes in those areas. In fact, they seemed to make even more mistakes than the others. How could the organizations that stumbled the most make the breakthrough transformations?

The seed of the answer came to me one day, not from my professional work but from my personal interest in myth and legend. The realization came to me when I was quite literally standing on the probable ruins of Camelot, at South Cadbury Castle in Devon County, England. I was looking out over the countryside, thinking of the great mythical quests: Sir Percival's quest for the Grail, Jason's quest for the Golden Fleece, and Psyche's quest to find Cupid.

Then it struck me. *The quest itself fuels breakthrough and transformation.* I wondered if this could be true whether the quest is mythical, historical or organizational. In every story that is told of a realized quest, a door opens to breakthrough, ultimately creating new vitality or restoring waning vitality. Why would the same not be true of organizations? Looking back on my client work, I could see the archetypal pattern of quest repeat consistently. When a quest was present (even if not named as such), organizations excelled at transformation. Conversely, when organizations simply followed programmatic steps, they achieved only pedestrian results. I now believe that the propensity to quest was the key differentiating factor.

A quest of any kind is not a simple fail-forward notion. Certainly, those on quests do face trials, fail, overcome and thereby build new capability. But a quest involves much more than a series of trials and errors. A quest is a four-part journey toward success, through discovery and renewal:

- The call to adventure
- The outward journey of discovery
- The return journey, mastering the breakthrough
- The arrival with the prize of renewal

I now believe that, contrary to the popular view, going on a quest is not a romantic notion. It is more like a biological human necessity. The brilliant physician and microbiologist Charles Pasternak identifies the propensity to quest as a fundamental and uniquely human drive. He argues that it is the one quality that differentiates human development from that of other primates. The ability to seek beyond immediate needs, to find what is over the distant hill, propels human development in every aspect of endeavor. Naturally, business organizations follow the same pattern.

Over and over, societies build their myths upon a motif of quest. That is because a quest represents the high point of human endeavor, the time when people have pursued something much bigger than themselves. The events that form the quest are remembered, retold and eventually embellished in legend.

Just consider the transcontinental journey of Lewis and Clark during Thomas Jefferson's presidency. That is a quintessential quest that Americans never tire of retelling. By telling this story to the next generation, they weave the true story into the fabric of America's national epic myth. The fact that myths portray quests does not diminish the extraordinary significance of an actual quest. Quite the contrary; this fact underscores the idea that quest comprises the bedrock of human activity. The idea that human activity is driven by our nature to quest — and the resulting potential to achieve great transformations — certainly extends into business organizations, as well.

Most organizations, even those attempting transformational change, block quests at both the individual and organizational levels. By setting up systems that ensure safety and protect the stability and equilibrium of the organization, they block the ability to undertake an adventure of exploration and discovery, even if that quest has the potential to return huge rewards. As political scientist Aaron Wildavsky points out in *Searching for Safety*, refusing to continue seeking is the most dangerous and destructive of behaviors.

Once I understood the pattern of the quest, I could see that pattern's unmistakable appearance throughout organizational transformations. At first, however, I considered its value to be only retrospective, as a tool for analyzing past change initiatives. I used the quest structure in this way for more than ten years, to help me assess complex transformations retrospectively.

Gradually, I added to my understanding of the quest through exposure to the writings of Joseph Campbell, FitzRoy Somerset (Lord Raglan), Christopher Vogler, John Matthews, Charles Pasternak, Jordan Peterson, and others.

As I gained a deeper understanding of the quest, I came to see it not as simply a great metaphor but as a powerful system for navigating transformations, regardless of the field of endeavor.

While this helped me see the pattern more clearly in existing transformations, it also allowed me to use the quest proactively, to

- Plan and launch complex transformations.
- Guide transformational leaders.
- Understand the progress of transformations.
- Determine next actions.
- Anticipate barriers.
- See the connections in seemingly random events.

All quests follow an essential pattern. Pathfinders set out on an adventurous journey of exploration and discovery, in search of a breakthrough element that will allow the pathfinders to heal an underlying cause of misfortune. It is a journey away from the everyday world, where things are known and agreed upon. The quest is a journey beyond the threshold of discovery, into uncharted territory where new potential abounds. While the path is rife with obstacles, those who succeed will realize vast rewards that were not accessible at home base.

In the context of an organizational transformation, a quest takes on an even richer and more faceted meaning. It is not fantastic dragons that you will be battling on an organizational quest. Your challenges will take place in the real world, though it can be every bit as adventurous. As a transformational leader, you will lead your organizational team into uncharted territory where the potential for new breakthroughs abound. You and your team of pathfinders will be tackling real-life obstacles in order to make a number of key discoveries on the way to a major breakthrough. With bold leadership, and by embracing the call of your quest, you can transform your organization – and sometimes change the world.

Parallel Quests

If you want to build a ship, don't drum up men to gather wood, divide the work, and give orders. Instead, teach them to yearn for the vast and endless sea.

— Antoine de Saint-Exupery,
World War II pilot and author of The Little Prince

The scientific paths of questing and discovery are often convoluted and have unexpected twists and turns. They have the same qualities that make fictional adventure stories interesting and readable.

— Baruch S. Blumberg, winner of Nobel Prize in medicine

Going on a quest is the opposite of staying at home base. Space shuttles are built to explore the wonders of space, not built to stay on the ground at Cape Canaveral. In the same way, bold leaders in organizations were never meant to stay in a safe but stagnating world where people say, "We've always done it this way." As a leader, you want to stretch the frontier, go beyond what is known, and discover what will help your organization thrive in years to come.

Epic myths and legends leap to mind when I talk about a quest. King Arthur's knight, Percival, searches for the Holy Grail that promises healing to a kingdom in danger of unraveling. Young Frodo goes on a quest to destroy a ring that wields dangerous powers. A quest begins with a feeling of unease, a sense that all is not right within the kingdom. In business organizations, this feeling could present itself in the form of a looming crisis, a sense of being stuck, or a need to restore vitality and create a way for the organization to renew itself.

That is my mission and the reason I created the quest approach. I believe the key to organizational transformation is releasing the vast unrealized potential of people. To do this I show them how to turn the present crisis into a call to adventure and then turn the call to adventure into a journey of discovery. I then guide them on that journey so they can move far beyond the threshold of their current practices to achieve breakthroughs that restore, in often unforeseen ways, the vitality of their organization.

When you decide that staying at home base has fewer benefits than taking your organization on a quest, you have begun an intentional adventure into the unknown, a journey that propels your organization forward, from a place of relative safety to a place of renewal. You will need to journey through a sometimes baffling wilderness. Obstacles may seem impenetrable, but as the quest continues, you can use your newfound capabilities to find your way through, ultimately reaching a place of breakthrough. The breakthrough can be so transforming that it creates a new way of functioning. With this breakthrough, you can bring renewal to the organization.

Modern-day stories in books and film echo the ancient quest. Indiana Jones hunts for the Holy Grail. Frodo quests for the means to destroy the powerful ring. Luke Skywalker searches for the means to destroy the Death Star.

These stories of fiction are fascinating, giving us a picture of the underlying pattern of all quests and hinting at what can actually be achieved by organizational quests. Heroic real-life adventures, such as Charles Lindbergh's quest to fly solo across the Atlantic or Ernest Shackleton's quest to save his crew in the Antarctic, reveal the same quest pattern, as well.

The Lewis and Clark Quest

I chose one true-adventure model to refer to throughout this book, a model that closely fits the quest model in organizations. It is the journey taken by the Corps of Discovery, led by Captains Meriwether Lewis and William Clark from 1803 to 1806.

Commissioned by President Thomas Jefferson to find a trade route to the Pacific Ocean, the Corps left the relative safety and comforts of St. Louis. From there, they traveled upriver on the Missouri River through the newly purchased Louisiana Territory and the much-disputed swath of land northwest of that, which was then called Oregon Country. Part of the mission of the Corps was to claim the disputed land for the United States. At issue was the fact that Oregon Country (which now comprises land including the northwestern states and part of southwestern Canada) was also at the time claimed by Spain, England, Russia and the Native people who lived there; no one was willing to give it up without retribution of some kind.

The Corps traveled through the territories of many tribes whose names were little known to Americans on the East Coast. After narrowly escaping grizzlies and winter starvation, the pathfinders came to their long-awaited place of discovery: the Columbia River's route to the Pacific. Though the Corps did not find an all-water route from St. Louis to the Pacific, they did bring back a viable trade route. Even more importantly, they brought back a sense of wholeness to the United States, a young nation that would soon stretch from the Atlantic to the Pacific.

There are no maps of the wilderness where you are headed. Lewis and Clark had no maps, either. In fact, they were charged by President Jefferson to make maps for those who followed. Because they did so, we can now trace their journey through this book. I can find strong parallels between their journey and those of a daring organization such as yours. When you compare your organization's quest to Lewis and Clark's quest for the Pacific, you can get a sense of the high adventure you will face along the way.

The Quest Effect

Success breeds conservatism, and that means a love affair with the status quo and an aversion to change.
— *Frank Popoff, chairman of Chemical Financial Corporation*

Is Conventional Wisdom Wrong?

Much has been written about business transformations and what it takes to make them successful. In my years as a business student, executive, business school instructor, and management consultant, I've read much of it and must admit that much of what has been written seems entirely reasonable.

Yet, what if it was essentially wrong? It seems preposterous, doesn't it? But, what if there was another element, largely invisible to leaders and management scientists? What if, when that element was present, the lightning of breakthrough transformation could strike again and again, yet without it, breakthroughs would be hit and miss at best? What if that element was well known in Western culture, but was obscured from businesses and organizations by arcane language?

My experience is that such an element exists and that it does indeed eclipse much of conventional wisdom about transformational change. That is what I want to share with you via this book. I call this element The Quest Effect.

The Quest Archetype

In 1949, acclaimed mythographer Joseph Campbell introduced a startling theory. By studying myths and legends from cultures throughout the world, Campbell determined that stories of the quest were evident in every culture. He observed that, while the details changed, the underlying pattern of the quest was virtually the same throughout the world's cultures. The quest is part of our universal collective view of the world. Campbell called the quest story the monomyth. It is the archetypal, universal pattern of the journey of transformation, with its structures and stages shared across wide-ranging times and places. The quest story illuminates the process of transformation and renewal in individuals, small groups and whole cultures.

But I want to move beyond the purely metaphorical treatment of the quest archetype. The quest plays out every day in all types of organizations, from manufacturing to healthcare to government. The Quest Effect is evident in a wide array of transformational initiatives including product development, quality movements, culture change, and strategic reframing, as well as entire industry transformations. In fact, the quest pattern has been evident in virtually every transformation I have studied.

I am proposing that the quest archetype is the elemental pattern for transformational change. Locked within the quest archetype is the prime pattern that captures the fundamental nature of transformation. The fact that the quest takes place in organizations every day is simply a reflection of the reality that organizations are in transformation every day.

Organizations rarely make the quest explicit. When they do, generally using a journey metaphor, it is expressed with vagueness or ambiguity, so the quest pattern is not easily apparent. When organizations quest without recognizing that they are doing so, the result can be a haphazard affair. They are not tapping the power of the quest archetype.

In myth and legend, the Knights of the Round Table undertook the quest for the Holy Grail, Jason and the Argonauts quested for the Golden Fleece, and Gilgamesh sought the secret to eternal life. In movies, the theme of quest is repeated: Dorothy journeys to find the Wizard of Oz, and Neo pursues the secret of the Matrix.

In history, as well, the theme continues through the centuries: Columbus searched for passage west from Europe to the Far East. Three hundred years later, Lewis and Clark quested for a route from the eastern United States to the Pacific. In the 1960s, NASA took up President John Kennedy's challenge to put a man on the moon within the decade. Quests, all of them.

I seek to encourage leaders to purposely pattern their transformation and breakthrough initiatives on the quest archetype. When they move from lack of awareness to intentional use of powerful quest structure, they will dramatically enhance their transformational capability, with the potential for breakthrough and renewal. In the rest of this chapter, I want to lay out the quest pattern concisely.

Meaning of the Quest

In the simplest terms, a quest is a search for or pursuit of something. However, for our purposes, we need a definition that captures a deeper meaning. In this deeper sense, a quest is a journey into uncharted territory for the purpose of exploration and eventual discovery of a prize or boon that, when returned, will revitalize the organization or heal a state of misfortune. It is often a perilous and uncertain venture, but it holds the potential for huge rewards or a game-changing breakthrough. While the path may be convoluted, the search is focused on the prize, not aimless wandering.

Organizations quest when they explore new territory, not when they follow the proven, business-as-usual path typified by steps programs. Organizational quests include:

- Thrusting into new markets
- Developing new families of products
- Creating new core processes
- Profoundly changing cultures

Start-up organizations quest continuously, but mature organizations rarely quest. Organizations that rarely or never quest will drift into decline.

What is the Quest Effect?

The Quest Effect is a phenomenon that takes place when pathfinders (individuals, teams or organizations) leave the safety of home base and explore uncharted territory in search of a prize that will renew the organization. The occurrence is marked by:

- A rapid increase in capability
- Tapping the creative wisdom of employees
- Contact with heretofore unexplored concepts and materials
- Discovery of a breakthrough
- A quantum jump in performance (a change of level)
- A significant renewal of the organization

When I contrast these outcomes with the accomplishments of others who pursued the same goals by using conventional planning, proven-path steps and accepted change management approaches, I see a remarkable difference. The traditional methods typically produce pedestrian results, while the quest results are often remarkable.

I want to be clear that I am not using the quest as a metaphor for some other change process. I am suggesting that organizations can literally pursue their own quests. They can use the archetypal pattern of the quest with fidelity. If they do, they can achieve their own prize: the means to renew the vitality of their organization. This is the Quest Effect.

Discovering the Quest Effect

As a management consultant, I spend my professional life helping leaders guide their organizations through significant transformations. In the beginning, I helped manufacturers adopt the Toyota Production System. I came armed with transformation plans, proven-path methodologies, powerful tools, and benchmarks from others who had achieved much. I am pleased to report that nearly all of my clients made meaningful gains — and a proportion of them made stunning breakthroughs. Of course, I wanted all my clients to move from meaningful gains to breakthroughs. That was the challenge that fueled my quest for a different approach.

Another challenge was getting the leaders and managers to moderate their use of best practices for change management. Many popular conceptions concerning how to manage during a transformation actually hinder the quest. Accepted ideas about planning, staffing, organizing, and project tracking were harmful and had to be discontinued or at least de-emphasized. It was clear that clinging to business-as-usual practices was not going to serve the organization in uncharted territory.

I observed how organizations that followed the quest pattern consistently achieved breakthroughs, while others, following more familiar approaches, were improving their business but not at breakthrough levels. They were extending their capabilities but not really transforming. Those who tried to manage their way through transformations using conventional techniques seemed significantly more conservative and risk-adverse. In contrast, the breakthrough organizations cut their ties to their business-as-usual world and created their own path, discovering what they could become and achieving breakthroughs that drove transformation. Organizations were not achieving breakthrough by following incremental, proven-path approaches.

My conclusion was that those who followed the quest pattern consistently achieved a different outcome: a higher order of capability and performance that was sufficient to create new sources of vitality and ultimately renew the organization. I observed a Quest Effect.

Making the Quest Proactive

The challenge is to make the Quest Effect actionable. I could observe the Quest Effect in retrospect, seeing how the quest played out in successful transformations. But I wanted to help leaders proactively create the Quest Effect to amplify their transformation results.

As it turned out, the answer was disarmingly simple (though quite counter-intuitive). It was about adopting the quest as the frame of reference for the transformation efforts. I began to explicitly use the stages and phases of a quest with clients. We adopted quest language — not the language of myth and legend — but still much different from the common language of change management. For example, language changed from phrases like *burning platform* or case for change to the *Call to Adventure.* We de-emphasized tasks, assignments, and due dates and focused on a journey of discovery, incorporating concepts like a compass, unexpected events, and spiral development. If the organization saw itself on a quest — and knew how to follow the quest way — it stood a very good chance of achieving breakthroughs.

Achieving the Quest Effect

Once I was aware of the possibility of a Quest Effect, I could observe the phenomenon at work in a multitude of stories about business breakthroughs and transformation.

One of my favorite stories is about General Electric's transformation. Instead of simply copying Motorola's groundbreaking work, GE used Motorola as an inspiration for its own exploration. They stood on Motorola's shoulders, borrowed principles and then charted a new path. The results were nothing short of world changing. Contrast GE's quest with the legions of organizations who have artlessly copied GE's model (as if it were a steps program) and who have not come remotely close to breakthrough results. GE was inspired by Motorola but discovered its own path to a breakthrough.

The GE story is a case of a dramatic example of the Quest Effect. One can see how the Quest Effect manifested itself in a successful transformation at GE, but failed to appear in lesser achievements of nearly all the imitators. The quest is a process of exploration and discovery, not a paint-by-numbers steps program.

When organizations deliberately use the quest model, they will achieve breakthrough results. Consider some results from organizations that have used the quest approach:

- Hospital corporation creates the fastest emergency department in the country and generates over $40 million annually in profitable new revenue.

- International airport moves from out of the ranking to number five in customer service among major airports in the world.
- Surgical service increases capacity by over twenty percent, while simultaneously shortening the surgical day by two hours.
- Cruise line radically changes customer booking experience and dramatically increases bookings.
- Bank increases loan-processing capacity five-fold with same resources.
- Hospital invents radical care management approach and reduces length of stay by forty percent.
- Insurance company creates a "disruptive innovation" product that opens a new market.
- Truck parts manufacturer doubles its output within two weeks.

I am convinced that you can achieve the Quest Effect in your organization. This book will show you the process. It asks you to choose boldness in taking on the adventure of the quest over holding on to the perceived safety of home base and the status quo. Look beyond immediate problems. Is there an underlying breakdown of the status quo? If so, you have an opportunity to launch a quest, discover a breakthrough, and renew your organization. That is the essence of the Quest Effect.

The Quest Journey

As to methods, there may be a million and then some, but principles are few. The man who grasps the principles can successfully select his own methods. The man who tries methods, ignoring principles, is sure to have trouble.

— *Ralph Waldo Emerson, American essayist*

At its heart, the quest is a journey, albeit a very special one. It is a journey with great purpose, a search for a marvelous prize. If you want to understand the process of the quest, the best place to start is with that journey. This book is organized according to a journey, because that is how the quest unfolds in organizations. Knowing how to apply the quest depends on where your team is on the journey. I have included two diagrams of the quest in this chapter and will refer to those diagrams in subsequent chapters.

While the details of each quest are unique, they all follow a fundamental pattern or archetype that you can decipher and use to your advantage. If you understand the quest archetype, you can draw on lessons from other quests, identify actions, anticipate threats and opportunities, know when it is time to press on to the next phase, and recognize when you are getting off course. Events that would otherwise seem chaotic will have a clear purpose. Understanding the fundamental pattern of the quest dramatically improves the possibility that you will achieve a breakthrough.

In contrast to the Eastern idea of a never-ending path, the quest, in its simplest form, is a journey out and a return journey home. The turning point is the attainment of a breakthrough that holds the power for healing or renewal or a new way of being.

On the outbound journey, pathfinders discover the prize; on the homeward journey they use the prize to transform and renew the organization. The completed quest takes the organization to a new level of functioning.

The journey out and the journey back are bisected by the Threshold of Adventure. This line distinguishes the everyday, business-as-usual world from unexplored territory. Pathfinders must cross this threshold when moving into uncharted territory and must cross again on the return journey when they return back to home base. When the Threshold of Adventure is combined with the outbound and return demarcation, the landscape of the quest becomes four quadrants. The pathfinders cross every quadrant of the quest landscape during their transformational journey.

Each quadrant represents a phase of the quest. I call the quadrants

1. Launch
2. Exploration
3. Breakthrough
4. Renewal.

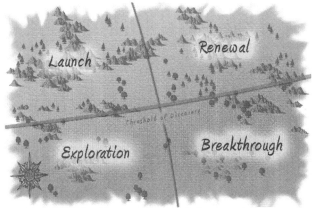

Figure 1: The four quadrants of the quest landscape

Phases of the Quest

Phase One: Launch

The Launch Phase, covering activities in the first quadrant, addresses the organization's response to the initial threat or opportunity through the launch of the quest. The Launch must awaken the organization to the fact that something has irrevocably upset the status quo. In this phase the organization must wake up to the threat or opportunity, overcome reluctance and break away and organize to launch. It must "unfreeze" the organization, in social psychologist Kurt Lewin's words, so that it can answer the Call to Adventure. If it falls short, the quest will fail to launch. Successful quests begin in the Launch phase and move into uncharted territory in the second phase.

The Launch Phase has several milestones:

1. Status Quo: enjoying initial stability
2. State of Misfortune: awakening to the threat or opportunity
3. Call to Adventure: sounding the call (and refusal to heed the call)
4. Meeting the Mentor: engaging the first guide
5. Pathfinders: organizing those who will embark on the quest
6. Holdfasts: breaking free from holdfast forces
7. Instrument of Power: preparing for the journey and acquiring survival tools

The key pitfall in Phase One is the failure to launch. The magnetic draw of home base is powerful. Those who break away to pursue the quest must overcome a variety of obstacles. Those who succeed in launching the quest, in spite of the obstacles, put their organizations on the path to breakthrough.

Phase Two: Exploration

The Exploration Phase encompasses the activities in the second quadrant. In this phase the pathfinders have moved away from home base, across the threshold of adventure and into uncharted territory. Uncharted territory refers to areas of exploration that are not part of the organization's working body of knowledge —uncharted territory is not known or agreed upon by the organization. Uncharted territory is rich with novelty, untested assumptions, innovation opportunities, and breakthrough ideas. It is also beset by obstacles, risks and barriers.

In this phase, the pathfinders are in a race against time to discover the prize—the breakthrough—that holds the power to renew the organization. They must challenge current assumptions, learn new principles, develop their capabilities, and follow their discoveries toward the big breakthrough. Exploration is marked by committing to change, discovering new ideas, testing possibilities, and preparing for the breakthrough.

The milestones in the Exploration Phase are

1. Crossing the Threshold: separation from business-as-usual world of home base
2. Orienteering: assessing situation and gaining traction for journey
3. Helpers and Allies: receiving often-unforeseen help
4. Path of Trials: experimenting,

overcoming obstacles and setbacks
5. Ultimate Test: prevailing over a great crisis and surviving the ultimate test

The major risk in the Exploration Phase involves the misuse of time. If the pathfinders take too much time their discoveries will be too late to help the organization. Conversely, if they fail to devote enough time to build the capability necessary to achieve the prize, then they will fall short of the needed breakthrough. The pathfinders must hold the tension between the need to move quickly and the need to explore thoroughly.

Here pathfinders must forgo the security of the tried and true for the adventure of exploration and discovery. The hardships are real, but so are the thrill of discovery and the satisfaction of growth. In exchange for the hardship and effort pathfinders create opportunity for immense rewards.

Phase Three: Breakthrough

The Breakthrough Phase, in the third quadrant, also takes place in uncharted territory. It begins with the achievement of the big breakthrough. The breakthrough represents a turning point, wrapping up expansionary exploration and refocusing the group on mastering the breakthrough and returning with the prize to home base. After finding the breakthrough, the pathfinders must integrate their discoveries and innovations, master the use of the breakthrough, and make it usable under conditions at home base. The pathfinders will continue to face difficult challenges and setbacks as they prepare their return to home base.

The key milestones in the Breakthrough phase include

1. The Great Discovery: achieving the breakthrough

2. Turning Point: starting the return journey
3. Mastery in Two Worlds: mastering the breakthrough
4. Race Against Time: returning to home base before time runs out

This phase is sometimes referred to as the dangerous return. There is a tendency for the pathfinders to relax, knowing they have achieved a breakthrough and assuming the homeward journey will be trouble-free. Just as most mountain climbing accidents happen on the descent, pathfinders are easily caught off guard by the perils in the return phase.

The pathfinders must overcome challenges in making the breakthrough ready for everyday use. During Breakthrough, pathfinders balance the tension between taking the time for mastery and the urgency of returning with the prize.

The Breakthrough Phase challenges pathfinders to

- Recognize that the Exploratory Phase has ended
- Turn for home
- Refine the breakthrough for everyday use
- Prepare for the prize's adoption

Phase Four: Renewal

The Renewal Phase covers the return of the pathfinders to home base and the benefit of the prize. Here the pathfinders act to share their breakthrough with the entire organization. They introduce the breakthrough and attempt the big change on a routine basis. The organization works to perfect the change in the everyday world. By spreading the breakthrough, the organization creates the new vitality and renewal.

This phase may be a minor part of the quest if the original field experiments just need to be sustained. On the other hand, this phase can be challenging and complex if the organization needs to spread the breakthrough across many groups and make local adaptations. The key challenge is to pass the breakthrough from the custody of the pathfinders to the sustaining organization. This can pose organizational, technical, and cultural challenges. The organization will also have to deal again with holdfast forces. When successful, the pathfinders will have successfully concluded their quest and can take their place within the new order.

Major milestones of the Renewal phase include

1. Sharing the Breakthrough: spreading the breakthrough throughout the organization
2. Transformation: enjoying a new level of performance; pathfinders take their place in the new order

The Renewal phase concludes a cycle of the quest and takes the organization to a new level of functioning. The organization is now poised for a new period of relative stability and equilibrium. Yet, eventually there will be another awakening, a new call to adventure, and an opportunity to move the organization through the never-ending quest spiral. However, if the organization locks onto the new order and denies future quests, it will stagnate and decline. This is the fate of most organizations. But organizations that build the quest into their cultural DNA can extend their vitality indefinitely.

Making the Quest Intentional

The quest embodies the fundamental, prime pattern of transformation and renewal. The process of the quest takes place in organizations every day, generally without their recognition. When organizations make the quest explicit and use the knowledge and principles proactively, they magnify the power of the quest. When the archetype is not understood, or is ambiguous or distorted, then the power of the quest is lost. Organizations that quest without recognizing the pattern experience a haphazard affair. Tools from home base are inappropriately commingled with the quest elements and other quest elements are overlooked altogether.

The ability to tap the power of the quest is based on awareness. Professor Jean Westcott points out that awareness precedes choice. Without awareness, we have no power.

This book seeks to encourage leaders to purposely pattern their transformation and breakthrough initiatives on the quest archetype. When they move from lack of awareness to intentional use of powerful quest structures they will dramatically enhance their transformational capability and the potential for breakthrough and renewal. The quest can become an established tool for organizational transformation and renewal.

The Quest Landscape

The quest progresses through milestones during each phase of the journey. A milestone is both a sub-phase and a critical juncture on the quest. As the quest moves through the four phases, pathfinders typically encounter most, if not all, of the milestones. The power of the quest comes from recognizing and anticipating these milestones. The milestones form the fundamental pattern of the journey. The specific actions and developments of your quest will overlay this pattern.

Knowing the phases and milestones is useful in every quest, even when the specific circumstances are vastly different. Understanding the landscape is the first step in being able to use a pattern of the quest to power transformational change in your organization. The chart in figure 2 depicts the quest journey and shows the milestones in each quadrant.

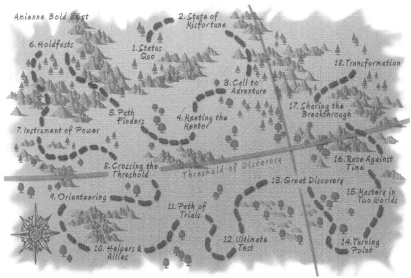

Figure 2: Quest Milestones

The order of the milestones is approximate; quests generally encounter the milestones shown in each quadrant, but the sequence is not hard and fast. Every journey is subject to unplanned events, setbacks, and discoveries that reframe the quest. The milestones are potentialities, not activities. They overlap, fade in and out, and change in intensity. Moreover, the journey can double back on itself, requiring the pathfinders to revisit previous milestones. You cannot cook-book the quest with the milestones, but you can use them to guide your way.

Use this map as a quick guide to the rest of this book. Each subsequent section and chapter is a description of a phase or milestone on the quest journey. In the following chapters, I describe the phases and milestones in both the archetypal and corporate form and guide you through the quest. Following the path in the map, I share important lessons from the quest, advise you of leadership challenges, warn you of pitfalls, and alert you to opportunities. It is my aim to encourage you to engage the quest, creating new opportunities to achieve breakthrough and renewal.

Phase One: Launch

In mature organizations, most justifiable quests are never launched. The almost compulsive need for safety, security, stability and equilibrium overrides the call to adventure. Therefore, Launch is not a simple organizing phase; it is a critical phase in your quest, the phase where most quests are stillborn. The challenges are great: recognizing the breakdown in the status quo, seeing beyond the presenting crisis, sounding a compelling call to adventure, finding a mentor, and putting together a team of pathfinders. When those challenges are met, you can launch the quest. How well you launch the quest is the single most important predictor of your success.

The chapters in this section guide you through the following milestones:

Status Quo

The status quo is the beginning point of the quest. It marks a period of relative stability and equilibrium. Stability does not necessarily imply prosperity; it can be a period of stagnation. It can also be a time of innocence when the organization is unaware of a pending opportunity or crisis.

State of Misfortune

The organization awakens to a present or imminent state of misfortune. The misfortune could be a closing window of opportunity, as well as a crisis situation. The state of misfortune threatens the status quo and could create critical instability. Sometimes a lone voice points to the problem that others have failed to recognize. At other times, an external event jolts the organization awake to the threat or opportunity.

Call to Adventure

The call to adventure acknowledges the state of misfortune. It also outlines the purpose of the quest, showing how it will relieve the misfortune or exploit an opportunity. The call creates a picture of what the organization can become. It also gives the organization an impetus to act.

Meeting the Mentor

Mentors or guides are people who have first-hand knowledge of the uncharted territory and the nature of the quest. Other helpers may appear later in the quest, but it is the first mentor who sets the stage for the quest and helps launch the journey. The organization may encounter the mentor before or soon after the call to adventure. The mentor can help craft the call to adventure, help the organization embrace the quest, and prepare the pathfinders.

Pathfinders

Following the call to adventure, leaders determine who will go on the quest. In myth, the pathfinders are often nascent heroes. The best pathfinders are passionate about the mission and engaged in the quest. Organizational leaders generally identify the pathfinders, create a team or teams, and assure that the team is capable before launching the quest.

Holdfasts

Every organization is replete with holdfast forces that seek to keep the pathfinders firmly rooted at home base, away from uncharted territory, especially in circumstances where the organization feels safe and secure. These forces are activated by risk. The job of the pathfinders is to break free of these holdfast forces to launch the quest. While presenting barriers, holdfast forces also serve to protect the status quo by discouraging ill-timed or misguided quests.

Instrument of Power

The instruments of power are the survival tools and techniques that will serve the pathfinders on their quest. Instruments of power are the real-world equivalent of the mythical magic amulet, sword of power, or cloak of invisibility. Pathfinders depending on these tools must know how to use them. Here the mentor will share knowledge with the pathfinders about the nature of the quest.

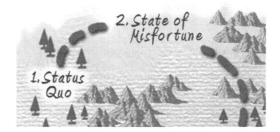

I. Status Quo

The manager accepts the status quo; the leader challenges it.
— Warren G. Bennis,
scholar and organizational consultant

Status quo, you know, that is Latin for "the mess we're in."
— Ronald Reagan, 40th U. S. president

In 1801, Thomas Jefferson becomes the third president of the new republic that stretches only as far west as the Mississippi River. Two-thirds of the citizens live within fifty miles of the Atlantic Ocean. Americans have the natural resources to support an unlimited zest for expansion and depend on that expansion for economic growth. Trappers continue to find new sources in the fur trade, an important source of the nation's wealth. Forest land is being cleared for agriculture. Immigrants are flowing in from all over Europe with the hope of a better life. Yet President Jefferson sees that the status quo can't hold for long. Jefferson's personal secretary is a man named Meriwether Lewis.

Recognize the Signs

In any system, such as the new nation of the United States of America in 1801, you can often detect a period of relative stability and progressive growth, a state of innocence and self-satisfaction. But catastrophe could be lurking nearby, for those who fail to recognize the signs.

The same holds true for those of us in business organizations that are operating like clockwork, with relative stability and prosperity. Think of the strategic mistakes of Digital Equipment in the computer business or Xerox in the copier business or GM in the auto business. No matter what the warning signs were outside the gates, the general feeling within the organization was that nothing could destroy the determination to hold onto and build upon what the company had already constructed.

You can hear the boasting confidence in King Arthur's voice near the beginning of the story of "Excalibur" as he asks Merlin, "Where hides evil in my kingdom, then?"

Merlin wisely responds, "Always... where you never expect it! Always!"

To be brought down by catastrophe, an organization surely doesn't need to be evil. Every business is prone to getting clobbered at some point by competition, wild market fluctuations, global changes in weather or government ... you name it. Organizations in the status quo phase say, "We've built Camelot and can deal with any crises as they come up. Everything's fine. We must avoid undue risk."

Pay Attention to Forces of Instability

Stability and prosperity are the fruits of past efforts and ongoing growth, improvement and refinement. You can envision moving up the more-or-less linear upward slope of the growth curve.

During the status quo period, there may be unplanned events and minor crises, but these do not normally threaten the stability and equilibrium of systems that produce prosperity. With proper attention, disaster is unlikely.

Nevertheless, the seeds of quest are often sown at this most unlikely time: when prosperity and stability set the tone for the organization. During the status quo period, organizations do pay careful attention to small crises, like brush fires, that threaten prosperity and stability. They stamp out these fires and then go back to business as usual. What they don't see are the underlying forces of the wasteland. Compare small crises (brush fires) to the wasteland (forest fires that threaten to wipe out whole cities over thousands of acres if something is not done to stop them). It's the threat of a wasteland, in addition to the smaller crises, that need to be addressed.

When times are good for a corporation, it is hard for most people to envision large crises that could overtake the organization. Yet that is exactly when potential wastelands need to be addressed. The forces of an unseen wasteland may already be undercutting future prosperity. Indeed, this is when prosperity needs to be protected for the long haul.

Periods of stability and prosperity can easily lead to a desire for safety. "We need to fortify our position," many will say, "so why not stick to the proven path?" Even in bad times it is hard to jump into the quest, but it is much harder for leaders to see that a quest is needed during times of prosperity. For most business executives, the more they have to protect, the more risk-adverse they become. A bias against risk in an organization can dim any interest in the quest. Mature organizations are the most vulnerable to the bias for safety. The temptation to suppress the quest can be overwhelming.

Beware the Lure of Safety

The quest is the means to restore vitality. Without it, organizations will opt for safety. They will choose what they already have, what they already know, and what they already agree upon. But too much safety is the road to ruin. Choosing safety over adventure is the path to organizational stagnation, decline, and eventual extinction.

Ironically, choosing safety — refusing the call to adventure — is the ultimate risk. One can see that by making consistent choices to stay safe, an organization will be stuck at home base, cut off from new sources of vitality, such as innovation, discoveries and challenging ideas.

Keeping an organization afloat by protecting the status quo won't help when a catastrophe or major interruption strikes. Strengthening an organization's culture won't help. In a crisis, it won't help to make small, measured improvements in processes, hiring practices or quality of service. Sometimes the status quo cannot be repaired, and a quest is the only path forward.

Questions for the Quest

1. How does present prosperity justify perpetuating the status quo?
2. Where are the disturbances or disruptions in the status quo?
3. What key assumptions and beliefs are not being challenged?

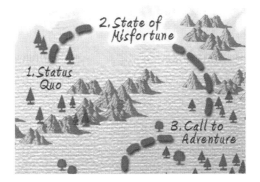

2. State of Misfortune

The shrewd guess, the fertile hypothesis, the courageous leap to a tentative conclusion – these are the most valuable coin of the thinker at work.

— Jerome S. Bruner, psychologist and educational theorist

Doing what's right is no guarantee against misfortune.

— William McFee, author of sea stories

At the very beginning of the nineteenth century, young Meriwether Lewis is growing agitated. As President Jefferson's private secretary, he is acutely aware that the United States is vulnerable to domination in North America by European powers. France, England and Spain have staked claims to territory in North America, and the westward expansion of Americans will soon run into boundaries claimed by these European powers.

More subtly, there is a spirit in America, a belief that individuals control their own destiny, and this belief clearly requires westward expansion. So far, the youthful United States is in no danger of being overtaken. Congress might be congratulating itself, saying, "We are handling our nation's small emergencies as they crop up; we have not lost anyone yet."

But the deep crisis or, in this case a window of opportunity, lies in the fact that the Louisiana Territory, which stretches across the wilderness, could possibly be purchased from France. If it is not purchased now, Spain can acquire it, thereby cutting off trade routes and territory across the West. But Jefferson needs to use all his shrewdness to make this deal go through. The Louisiana Purchase could double the size of the United States, but even if it could be purchased from France, does America have the means to assert its claim over the territory?

Be a Bold Leader

Meriwether Lewis was a bold leader — as well as a pathfinder — for his organization, the United States. He spent many evenings discussing with President Jefferson the encroaching European nations that threatened to forever confine his country to the East Coast of North America. With the strong sponsorship of President Jefferson, he looked ahead to see what opportunities could come from these unfortunate circumstances. As he and Jefferson consulted, they must have wrestled with these issues together, saying something like this: "Minor emergencies crop up everywhere around us, and it is hard not to put all our energies into these things. But what can be done to make sure the United States becomes a stronger nation and is not confined to one edge of this continent?"

As a business consultant, I often hear my clients asking similar questions of their circumstances:

"Our hospital's emergency department is no worse than any other in the city. We haven't lost anybody in the waiting room yet. But I look at the overcrowding and the people spilling out into the parking lot, and I have to believe there's a better and safer way to treat patients."

"Our online store is always busy. We're making money. But half the day is wasted with aggravating delays in orders, and our customer service department is getting the message that we don't respond to client needs as effectively as our competitors do."

"We do great for an airport our size, but our facility is almost 30 years old. In spite of that, how can we become one of the top airports in the world for customer service?"

If you have been questioning your circumstances in this way, you may be in the running for the position of pathfinder for your organization. There's just one glitch. Most of your associates focus on the ongoing minor emergencies and overlook the core problem, the underlying state of misfortune.

If nothing is done about the core problem, the organization will stall, stagnate and eventually collapse. You may not be the CEO or a recognized leader in the business, but you may become aware of the state of misfortune that underlies the minor emergencies that others focus on. You may be the one who can see the suffering that this state of misfortune causes, or will soon cause, for your fellow employees and customers. If you are a change agent, you want the organization to adapt and thrive. You feel passionate about this; you *must* do something about it.

A state of misfortune starts as a nearly unnoticeable disturbance. There seems to be a state of "stuckness" that keeps the organization from realizing its full potential. For the United States in 1801, the western border seemed to be stuck only a few hundred miles from the Atlantic Ocean. Without the purchase of the Louisiana Territory, Jefferson and Lewis knew that the United States could never reach its potential as a world power that stretched from the Atlantic to the Pacific.

Most organizations are stuck somewhere far from their full potential. When the stuckness persists, the organization loses its vitality — its ability to restore itself and endure in the face of change. Stuckness shows up in many ways. The organization may lose the edge in a key competency or lose competitive strength. The delivery systems may lag in their capability. Sometimes the cultures become toxic. Always, the work lives of employees become less meaningful and more difficult.

Feeling stuck will eventually result in a deep crisis or series of crises (a threat or a loss of a major opportunity) where decisive leadership is needed if it is to avoid a catastrophe. Faced with a deep crisis, you may think that your organization's only available option is to retreat to what is safe and proven. Yet, as I mentioned in the chapter on status quo, seeking safety may avoid the immediate crisis, but it will only deepen underlying conditions and spawn new crises.

Anticipate the Downturn

Pathfinders are the heroes we cheer for in adventure movies and in history books. Nothing would be possible without them, but they come to the forefront seemingly by accident, based on circumstances and timing, and they often rise out from the everyday world. Dorothy Day was a working-class single mother during the Depression, but she founded the Catholic Worker Movement, starting a groundswell of nationwide support for social justice. Luke Skywalker was a simple young farmer on a distant planet, but he led a cosmic battle against the forces of evil. And Lewis, still in his early twenties, was asked to leave his Virginia cabin for the halls of the President at his home in Monticello.

Before taking on their mantles, though, bold leaders may be the ones to see a crack in prosperity before anyone else does. They discover a crack in the system when revenues are still rising and growth is strong. Other people in the organization acknowledge the problem later, when they finally see enough proof that the organization's star is on the decline. By that time, however, it may be too late. That's why you need to act before the downturn, before the slump becomes a freefall.

In the same way, you, as your organization's bold leader, know that in order to thrive in years to come, your company needs to begin the quest soon, even if it is currently on a path of prosperity. If you have talked with others in your company about seeking a new way, you know that breaking away from the norm will not be a popular view. The new path will lead the pathfinders into the unknown. The unfamiliar path is always an intimidating place. But quest is the only way to make a breakthrough. If you handle it well, your journey through the unknown can take your company to new levels of performance, leading to a vital transformation.

Look Beneath the Minor Emergencies

When you observe a growing disruption in your organization, that's when you need to look for the underlying state of misfortune. What is causing this disruption? These troubling feelings can be signs of a looming crisis.

Systems theorist Ervin Laszlo described how minor disruptions or instabilities, when left unchecked, can get out of control, leading to instability for the whole system. Bifurcations— various attempts to transition the business— are often failures; the system collapses. Yet sometimes, the attempt is a breakthrough and the system experiences a quantum leap that will bring it to a higher order of performance. When restoration attempts are random, breakthroughs are rare. The purpose of a quest is to make systematic attempts at a breakthrough, dramatically improving the organization's chances of transforming to a higher-order system.

Watch bold leaders in other organizations. They are the people who stand out because of their adventurous spirit and attraction to new and unconventional ideas. They are the first to reveal the misfortune and give clues as to what the future could hold. I recall that one of my clients at a hospital noticed that one hand surgeon ran his cases on time and was able to turn over his operating room quickly while the rest of the surgical department started cases late and wasted time on room turnover. The client wondered aloud if the hand surgeon could be giving the hospital a glimpse of its potential future. An Internet technology client of mine noticed that one project, run outside the formal system and without the controls that were otherwise required, was the only project to come in on time and on budget. Could the rest of the organization use a similar approach? Bold leaders use these glimpses to point the way to a future breakthrough.

To find out what the bright future could hold for your organization, look past the momentary emergencies and consider your organization's customers and employees. Ask yourself, who is suffering? Who are the people in need here? How can we resolve the issues so they are helped?

The responsibility of the bold leader, at this point, is to discern the underlying state of misfortune and appreciate its impact. To paraphrase what Merlin wisely advised Arthur at this point, "Relax – do nothing – feel the power of your newfound understanding."

At this point, don't call a meeting of the board. Don't even try to garner support from the water cooler crew. David Spangler's advice in *The Call* is to be quiet when faced with this stage of an adventurous journey. There's no need to flail around, creating havoc. The early stirrings of understanding will get louder as you go along, turning into a call to adventure. If you understand the complete problem immediately, then you may be undergoing a specific minor crisis, not a full-fledged state of misfortune. If this is the case, try to take your understanding deeper. Make sure that you understand the underlying state of misfortune before sounding the call to your adventure.

Of course, the state of misfortune may be abundantly apparent to all – the result of a wrenching upheaval. This happens when products fail, processes break down, opportunities expire and a myriad of other disruptions. In this case, your job as a bold leader is to put words to the state of misfortune and sound the call to adventure.

Be fit for more than the thing you are now doing. Let everyone know that you have a reserve in yourself, that you have more power than you are now using.

— *James A. Garfield, 20th U.S. president*

Questions for the Quest

1. What weaknesses could kill your organization?
2. What are the underlying connections between recent minor emergencies? Is there an underlying state of misfortune that is creating emergencies?
3. Can you describe the state of misfortune in your organization?
4. Is there a window of opportunity that your organization must exploit?
5. Who is suffering or will suffer if you organization fails to act?

6. What unchallenged assumptions perpetuate this state of misfortune?
7. What would it take to heal the conditions that create the state of misfortune?

3. Call to Adventure

Be careful going in search of adventure — it's ridiculously easy
to find.

— William Least Heat-Moon, author of *Blue Highways*

*As soon as the United States purchases the Louisiana Territory in 1803,
the stage is set for the exploration of the western part of the continent, well beyond
the safe towns along the Missouri River. To avoid alarming the European powers,
President Jefferson quietly asks Congress to fund the Expedition and is granted the
funds. Jefferson formally asks Lewis in a letter to lead a westward exploration of
North America, to find an all-water trade route and describe what America had
just bought in the Louisiana Purchase. In heeding the call, Lewis becomes the initial
pathfinder of the adventure.*

Pathfinders Need to be Open to the Call

In all adventures, an expedition begins with a call. The call to adventure urges a pathfinder to leave the everyday world of the organization, giving the impetus to take action. As a result, the pathfinder can commit to the adventure and begin taking steps that will separate him or her from the security of home base.

There is probably no clearer call to adventure than the one Jefferson gave Lewis that day in 1803: Follow the Missouri River up to its headwaters, and from there find a water route to the Pacific. In your organization today, you might wish you could hear just such a clarion call, followed by specific guidance and, of course, funds to finance your journey. Often, though, the call to adventure is indistinct, so quiet that at first you could easily ignore it. Contrary to what happened when Jefferson made the call to Lewis, resources to finance a venture like yours will not be dropped in your lap, and it is very likely the call will not come from the president of your organization. But the louder the call becomes, the more it attracts the pathfinder if he or she chooses to stay open to adventure.

You don't have to be a top leader in the organization to answer the call. A pathfinder could be as ordinary as a knight in a fairy tale, which is to say, not that ordinary at all. The pathfinder takes on an extraordinary job. You can think of everyday pathfinders from history and fiction.

Former slave Harriet Tubman never attended a conference on leadership training, but she answered the call to adventure and led thousands of slaves to freedom. Young Luke Skywalker attended no Top Gun School on his planet, yet he led a danger-filled mission to destroy the enemy and save the universe. Virtually anyone in a corporation who answers the call to adventure can become part of a pathfinding team that travels through uncharted territory and carries back a prize that will ultimately revitalize the organization.

What is the call to adventure? How do you know when you hear it? Most importantly, how do you respond? According to author Toby Johnson, "The call to adventure begins with a remarkable event or an insight that reveals to the hero that he or she has discovered something about life." In the corporate quest, you, a soon-to-be pathfinder, discover something about the organization. You see the possibility of a higher order of function — and that vision gives power to the call to adventure. No more are you tied to thinking that your work does not matter. Indeed, the work is now to help change the world.

Your adventure that could change the world may be a relatively simple idea, a plan so straightforward that it has been overlooked in the past.

In Detroit, I was asked to visit a large hospital's emergency department (ED). The department, which had already spent several million dollars in renovations, was the only ED in the area with 100 percent private exam rooms. It was a state-of-the-art facility. The hospital had commissioned four consulting engagements in the past seven years and was complying with almost all of the recommendations. The ED had made many expensive improvements, but it was still unable to address the underlying state of misfortune.

The ED was experiencing severe overcrowding, extreme wait times, and excessive total visit times. The waiting room was packed so full that people overflowed into the parking lot. People who came and saw the crowd often just left without being seen. Ambulances were diverted to other hospitals because of overcrowding. Moreover, the unfavorable word of mouth in the community kept people from even contemplating coming to the ED at all.

Everything seemed so complicated and the consultants' reports didn't help – they were dense and complex in themselves. Yet, while we talked, the underlying simplicity of the problem came into focus. People who were suffering were not just the ones in the waiting room. The ED had become a bottleneck for the entire hospital, keeping patients with urgent needs from being admitted to the hospital itself.

The solution was a simple concept: make the pipeline into the hospital bigger so people in the community could get care both in the ED and the hospital. Once one employee, Connie, grabbed hold of this simple concept, she needed to sound the call to adventure. She sounded the call to adventure and great things happened. Her story became well known and, as a result, she changed the way emergency care was delivered around the world.

Get Off the Burning Platform

Sometimes no clarion call is needed. Some organizations find themselves wrenched into uncharted territory, the result of a sudden interruption in the status quo. The great British explorer, Ernest Shackleton was thrust onto his quest to save his crew the day his ship was crushed by ice in the middle of the Arctic Ocean. Standing on an ice floe without a ship, he calmly told his crew, "Now we will go home." As a bold leader, you may simply need to provide hope when the situation seems desperate.

Sometimes the call comes from outside the walls of the organization, threatening to upset the stability within. You have seen the movies where the pathfinder stands on a burning platform of some kind — a ship or a building — and is forced to act immediately or lose everything. Losing that opportunity may result in a disaster that will descend not only on the pathfinder, but also on the entire organization.

In Portland, Oregon, two nurse managers were standing on a virtual burning platform. They were about to hear the call to embark on a quest that would change the world of medicine, though in all probability, no one had any idea they would do so. Alicia Super and Sylvia McSkimming worked at Providence Medical Center, a major hospital in Portland. When Oregon passed its death-with-dignity law, saying that doctors had the right to help patients die, the administration at Providence recognized that the law violated its Catholic mission, to honor life. Providence decided to continue on as before, making no new policies about the right to die.

But the two nurse managers saw a second option. The business-as-usual answer would have been to go on as if nothing had happened. Instead, they sounded a call to adventure, urging the hospital, and other Catholic hospitals, to consider another path. They said that death with dignity could be based on Catholic values. They identified the people who were suffering as those who were in dire pain or those who were not alert enough to complete the end-of-life process. They saw a higher-order mission for their hospital to alleviate the suffering of that group. Their call to adventure was to discover a more dignified end-of-life experience. Their quest eventually changed the practice of end-of-life medicine in the United States.

The nurse managers worked with Providence to change the end-of-life care for many of its patients. They went on to found the organization that set the standard for end of life care: The Coalition for Compassionate Care.

Then the two were instrumental in the American Medical Association's decision to consider creating a new medical specialty: palliative care (soothing symptoms without effecting a cure). Even though AMA eventually voted it down, every physician is now more aware of the possibilities of palliative care. Many physicians now specialize in palliative medicine.

In your organization, you may be presented with a quest opportunity. No matter how the call to adventure comes to you, your job as a bold leader is to create an opportunity to move the organization to action. You must decide if the situation requires a radical approach, not just managing the little crises. You can choose to use this chance to transform the business.

Discern if the Call is Real

You can choose to answer or deny the call to adventure. In stories, the pathfinder may deny the call or refuse to answer it with action. The call can be an unwelcome arrival when it disturbs the pathfinder's comfort level. For a while, the pathfinder may be able to delay answering the call or attempt to refuse the call all together. However, the call may not simply fade away. Sometimes seeing the subtle crisis building will haunt the pathfinder like a curse, increasing anxiety. No longer can the pathfinder be satisfied with the status quo. Refusing the call has consequences that may become intolerable. Eventually, to relieve the disquiet, the pathfinder may choose to answer the call. But if left unanswered for a long time, the call to adventure will fade, and the opportunity for adventure will be lost. This is the raw material of organizational "stuckness."

You may be wondering, "How do I know when it's time?" If you are asking that question, then the moment for change is upon you. It has presented itself, and you need to choose whether or not to accept the call. You might think you were flying under the radar, but now you are caught in the crossfire of change. Committing to the adventure is essentially a decision to act in the face of uncertainty. Commitment means deciding to launch, or asking others to launch, an exploration that has no clear outcome and is often dangerous, disturbing, and uncomfortable. Answering the call will take you far from the safety of home base. However, the potential rewards of such a journey are immense. Besides, refusing the call means adapting to diminishment.

Be the Leader who Sounds the Call to Adventure

Are you the one to sound the call to adventure? You can use the following as a test:

- You feel a disturbance, a sense of unease, in the organization.
- You can sense a great threat to the organization.
- You have the feeling that the organization has been ripped out of its comfort zone.
- You feel an overpowering personal calling connected to the purpose of the organization.
- You've caught a glimpse of how things could be spectacularly better.
- You can see how refusing the call is not working—and may even be causing harm.
- Some key has been revealed to you, and you must share it.
- You can see, when others cannot, that the window of opportunity is closing.

If any of the above causes a strong emotional reaction, then you may be the leader who will sound the call to adventure.

How to Sound the Call

If you are the one who must sound the call for others to answer, then you must set the quest in motion by triggering a desire that overcomes the aversion to risk and desire to escape the situation by seeking a safe harbor. You must create urgency and call the organization to immediate action. Your call must make it clear that the situation has changed; your organization needs to move to a new and highly desirable destination. Let others know that the way is not known — it needs to be discovered. To engage others, appeal to higher purpose (for example, to help those who are suffering). Show how a quest is the destiny of the organization ("If not us, who will help them?")

Make it clear how the crisis at hand is symptomatic of a deep problem or state of misfortune. Paint the destination as completely as possible, using several senses to describe it. Do not rely solely on a burning-platform case for change. The motivating power of the burning platform diminishes as the quest proceeds. Depend instead on a highly desirable future state to motivate the quest.

Do not rely on financial numbers except as a footnote to the call to adventure. Avoid excessive bravado. This is a time for humility prompted by higher purpose. Keep the means open; the quest is a path of discovery. Specifying the means now will only kill spirit. In short, make sure your call to adventure draws a bright line between the state of misfortune and renewal in the future.

Tell your call to adventure as a story. That's what bold leaders do. Describe what triggered the call, reveal the source of your unease with the status quo, tell why refusing the call has not worked for you, describe how the game has permanently changed, and show

how the window of opportunity is closing. Finally, paint a picture of how past events and the present situation have perfectly positioned the organization for the quest. The call to adventure is the single most important act of a bold leader. Make the effort to craft a compelling story.

Refusing the call to adventure and turning back are the stuff that tragedies and empty lives are made of. Listen to your dreams, make a commitment, take action.

— James Bonnet, story consultant, author of Stealing Fire from the Gods

Questions for the Quest

1. How has the situation in your organization been changed irrevocably?
2. How will people benefit if you or your organization answers the call to adventure?
3. What can your organization achieve, that is bold and new, by engaging the quest?
4. What are the rewards for a successful journey?
5. Why should others join you on the quest?

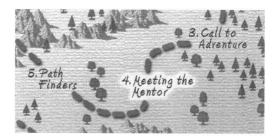

4. Meeting the Mentor

Trust one who has gone through it.

—Virgil, classical Roman poet

When Meriwether Lewis needs to choose a mentor for the journey, he calls upon William Clark, whom Lewis has accompanied before on missions in the U.S. Army. In fact, Clark was senior to him in years and had actually been his military superior when they last met. Nevertheless, for this cross-country quest, Clark readily accepts an equal position with Lewis, even agreeing to Lewis' astonishing proposal of sharing a co-captainship for the expedition. Chosen in large part for his mountain man expertise, Clark turns out to be a perfect match for Lewis on the journey.

Even though Clark has had little or no experience up the Missouri River beyond the normal bounds or across the mountain ranges, he has considerable experience beyond the threshold of civilization as woodsman, boatman and excellent communicator with Indian tribes. Just as important, Clark knows how to lead troops so they can survive as a tight band, alone in the wilderness for several years. The two leaders form an extraordinary alliance, with Clark as Lewis' mentor on the journey.

Mentors Help Launch the Journey.

While many guides may appear and withdraw during the course of an adventure, it is the first mentor, a helper or guide, who helps set the stage for the quest and helps launch the journey. On your organizational quest, your mentor could be a top leader, a consultant, or anyone who has experienced a quest and is willing to guide others.

Though President Jefferson set up the quest for Lewis, he allowed Lewis to go out on his own to find his mentor, William Clark. As in the case of Clark, the pathfinder and the guide can be embodied in the same person at times during your quest. Never as charismatic as Lewis, Clark chose to be a quietly direct influence on Lewis. Perhaps Lewis would never have completed the journey without Clark's steady guidance and friendship. Consider a mentor who has made an impression on you in a story, either in fantasy or in a real-life account. Here are three mentors for famous pathfinders:

The shaman-wizard Merlin helped Arthur realize his worth and trained him for great endeavors while Arthur was still an unknown. In much the same way, Wizard Obi wan Kenobi helped Luke Skywalker. Teacher Anne Sullivan helped Helen Keller reach beyond what was, at the time, considered impossible for someone who was both blind and deaf; Keller became an author, lecturer, and activist for the blind. Though there were other guides along the way, these were the first mentors for three pathfinders as they began their great adventures.

Mentors are commonly sages who possess unknown information that the companions will need in order to be successful on their quest. Anne Sullivan, for example, held the mysterious key of sign language, which launched Helen's journey.

Mentors may set up the quest but, somewhat surprisingly, they often do not accompany the pathfinder on the quest. Both Obi wan Kenobi in "Star Wars" and Glinda the Good Witch in "The Wizard of Oz," stayed behind but encouraged their pathfinders by appearing to them on the trail as if in dreams. The mentors for the troubled Apollo 13 mission were the engineers at Mission Control in Houston, not the astronauts circling the moon.

Find Mentor Qualities You Can Work With

In your quest, you will need to find a mentor whose qualities mesh well with your own. While we normally think of mentors as people, they could also take the form of a guidebook, an inspirational story or an internal voice. The most important aspect of mentors is that they have experience beyond home base. It's the mentor who draws on past quests, setting and adjusting the expectations of the pathfinders who are engaging the new quest.

It is not possible that your mentor has experienced the exact course that you, as pathfinder, will take. After all, if the guide had been there already, the land before you would not be uncharted territory. But the guide does know the territory in general and is on familiar terms with the nature of adventure.

Mentors can be your indispensable helpers, especially at the beginning of the journey when you are coming into awareness of the power of the quest. Your first guide may challenge you to step up to the call to adventure, and then help sound the call to adventure to others. They help you assemble companions for the journey, acquire instruments for power and survival, and equip you and your companions. They may even do battle or advise you how to battle with the holdfast forces and threshold guardians (see Holdfast Forces and Crossing the Threshold chapters).

Pathfinders without the protection of a mentor may fail at the threshold of discovery because they lack the insight and connections that the mentor has established over time on the other side. Early on, a pathfinder may not yet understand how to manage the environment just beyond the threshold. A good mentor will help you successfully launch your quest.

Mentors often have qualities that differ greatly from the normal characteristics of a leader. (Consider the offbeat mentorship role taken by Doc Brown in the movie "Back to the Future.") It's not uncommon for first guides to have an odd transcendent quality or wisdom. They can be difficult to understand, because they are prone to using structures and language from the other side of the threshold. They may be highly self-differentiated, to the point of eccentricity. They are often gifted people who have been underestimated, but come into their own in the mentor role.

Your mentor becomes somehow very connected to your quest. Your first guide can be a non-anxious presence in a very stressful situation. The mentor will be the first one to challenge you to overcome your victim mentality. In contrast to you as pathfinder, the mentor may be dispassionate, actually more interested in developing you the pathfinder than achieving the ends of your quest. Your inner development, of course, could actually help you achieve the ends of the quest, and perhaps the first guide knew that all along.

Watch Out for False Mentors

In your organization, beware the guide who is pushing a steps program (a programmatic approach), because a steps program cannot possibly work in an unknown environment. Be cautious of the guide who suggests taking the entire organization on the quest (typically with a wall-to-wall training approach). The whole-group approach worked for Moses, but it will almost certainly not work for you. A few good pathfinders are better than an oversized contingent.

Unfortunately, mentors may be conflicted about whether to help the pathfinder or whether to go about achieving their own ends. The two roles may coincide, but when they don't, conflict can arise. Be sure you understand the mentor's aims and understand how you can both achieve your objectives by working together.

Be Open to an Encounter

Your encounter with your mentor could happen seemingly by chance. Your mentor may identify you as a pathfinder candidate, someone of potential who is worthy of being mentored, and approach you. Or you could search for a mentor, based on a recommendation or personal experience. Look for a mentor who will push you and encourage your adventure, whether or not you feel ready. As former pathfinders, mentors are aware of the dangers, but don't expect mentors to remove risk. Their job is to help you face the risks and act boldly.

Questions for the Quest

1. Why might you need a mentor for your quest?
2. How will you discover what you don't know?
3. What can you learn from a mentor?
4. Who would be on a list of possible mentors for your quest?
5. Do you already have contact with a mentor without recognizing the opportunity?
6. If no candidates are coming to mind, where could you find a mentor?
7. What does the mentor want? How can the mentor fulfill his or her own needs?

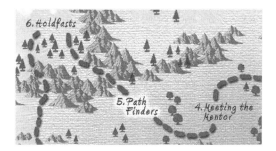

5. Pathfinders

We're not home-and-hearth people. We're the adventurers, the buccaneers, the blockade runners. Without challenge, we're only half alive.

— Alexandra Ripley, author of *Scarlett*

Lewis and Clark spend weeks gathering an energetic team of companions for their quest. The group eventually becomes known as the Corps of Discovery. The companions consist mainly of strong Army recruits from various forts. Many possess wilderness skills such as hunting, though none have traveled the westward route the Corps will take. All demonstrate their passion for the quest.

Gather Companions

Contrary to our popular Western notions of individual quests — which conjure images of fearless John Wayne types galloping out alone into the wilderness — the quest we are talking about is rarely accomplished without colleagues. As a bold leader, you need companions, fellow questers, to achieve the revitalizing ends of the quest. Jason had the Argonauts on the unknown sea. King Arthur had the Knights of the Round Table in England.

Dorothy had the scarecrow, tin man and lion in Oz. And Lewis and Clark led the Corps of Discovery in North America. Companions are essential to the success of any quest, because the obstacles encountered are too great for any one individual. So it's essential that you gather an excellent group of companions for your expedition.

As a leader of pathfinders on your quest, you will call on a group of companions at crucial times during the journey. You will draw on each companion's special expertise in subjects that are vital to achieving the goals of the quest. Your companions will carry the torch of leadership during critical passages. Your companions, regardless of their special expertise, should share not only in the glory of the breakthroughs but also in the mundane, pedestrian work of the journey. Without mutual assistance, the quest will be in danger of collapse. Protecting each other and keeping the party safe through a number of pitfalls is a fundamental job of every pathfinder.

Most important of all is passion for the quest. Passion creates the energy needed to progress through the journey. Without each companion's passion, the party will fall prey to diminished energy and victim mentality, which can spell death to the adventure. A heroic attitude drives your companions to find ways to overcome the barriers they will undoubtedly encounter and complete the journey in spite of those obstacles.

If a quest is a race against time across uncharted territory, then delaying it to assemble a dream team of companions is a risky action. You can, however, take actions to assemble companions with the qualities needed on the quest.

Sound the Call to Adventure to Attract Others

The best way to assemble companions is to encourage them to self-identify, to see themselves as connected to the nature of the quest. Remember that you, the initial pathfinder, were encouraged to risk the journey by hearing a call to adventure. The way to encourage others to join you is by sounding your call to adventure. Sounding your personal rendering of the call allows potential companions to connect your call to their personal passion. For example, Antarctic explorer Ernest Shackleton is said to have sounded this call to adventure in a classified ad in a London newspaper:

Men wanted for hazardous journey. Small wages, bitter cold, long months of complete darkness, constant danger, safe return doubtful. Honor and recognition in case of success.

According to many accounts, more than 5000 people showed up on the dock, ready to suffer hardship and risk their lives to join the Shackleton quest. Though the advertisement has never been conclusively proven to be Shackleton's, the story remains a strong reminder of how powerful an adventure call can be. When inviting companions on your quest, go beyond even Shackleton's call to adventure, and remember to

- State the higher purpose.
- State the time appropriateness and time urgency.
- Clarify the potential risk and hardship.
- Identify the prize that is the object of the quest.
- Refer to the immense rewards, should the quest be successful.

Use Passion as the Prime Consideration for Including Companions

I ask my clients to conduct a large-group event, where the group will deal with issues associated with the call to adventure, the state of misfortune, big opportunity or another element of a quest.

Toward the end of that event, I will ask people to step forward and identify their interest in pursuing the matter after the conclusion of the event. I'm looking for those people who feel some passion around the subject to be candidates for pathfinders on the quest. I consider subject-matter expertise secondary to passion. Those who stand up and self-identify are the ones to consider. Appointing subject-matter experts who have no passion is bad policy

Use Trust as a Key Criteria for Inclusion in the Party

Favor those you already know and trust, and exclude those you do not fully trust, even if your reasons seem unfounded. Because successful completion will depend on mutual assistance, particularly at critical junctures on the journey, trust is essential. As a leader, you often cannot know every companion at the outset, so work to build trust with everyone as the party of companions develops. This advice, however, must not be interpreted as justification to exercise prejudice against groups of individuals.

Prepare to Launch Without Everyone You Need to Complete the Quest

Just as Charbonneau, Sacagawea and Pomp joined the Corps of Discovery after it had left the quest's home base of St. Louis, key pathfinders may need to join your quest after it is underway. Waiting to form the perfect party of companions could be disastrous if it results in excessive delays; their expertise will be worthless if the quest falls short of completion. Moreover, the companions you need will not always be available at home base. The pathfinders you need most may be located beyond the threshold of discovery. In organizations, if you make your quest known, others will seek you out and offer assistance and some will offer to join the quest at just the right moment.

Travel Swiftly, and Travel Light

There is no room for those who aren't dedicated to the quest. All must be keen for the journey and ready to carry their share of the load. Political or sentimental assignments can kill the quest. It's the responsibility of the sponsor and the quest leader to make sure the party remains small and swift. While Lewis was gathering his provisions on the East Coast, a most prominent doctor asked to join the Corps on its journey. But Lewis wisely understood that a city doctor without wilderness experience would bog down the trip. So he declined the offer from one of the leading doctors of the age, learned what he could from him in the days available, and did the work of a doctor himself on the trail, including minor surgery and dispensing of medication.

Pathfinder teams need to travel fast and light; otherwise, they bog down. I once worked with a large information technology group that used a total of three pathfinder teams in an attempt to develop a new delivery system. I asked for five members on each team; after some compromise, we started with seven. But new members kept showing up, saying their bosses had sent them. Each new member claimed a special, "absolutely required," expertise. Within four weeks the three teams had bloated to between twelve and fourteen members apiece. The pace of the teams slowed to a crawl, and the teams eventually delivered pedestrian results, lacking in innovation. Make sure that every companion can help with the core work of the quest and can master one or more survival techniques.

Decide if You Need a Specialist

Though your pathfinder team needs to be small, it may still need a specialist. If your quest requires expertise in a certain area, find someone who would bring those specialized skills to your party. Shackleton brought a photographer, a cook and several navigators on his quest. Lewis and Clark realized that an interpreter would be useful throughout their expedition. Pathfinders with specialized jobs may need to bring along specialized survival tools for your quest.

Always be careful, however, not to let the size of your quest party grow out of control. No team member can afford to be just a specialist. Everyone will need to make a broad contribution, in order to keep the team small. In a quest I facilitated regarding operating-room-turnover redesign, a surgical redesign team relied on the sterilization technician for guidance on use of the autoclave and automated instrument-tracking technologies. However, that technician also helped with many other aspects of the new design.

Avoid Second Guessers

While you may be entirely committed to the quest, your companions may encounter second thoughts after joining. In the case of Lewis and Clark, the Corps experienced desertions and serious challenges to the captains' authority in the first weeks of the expedition. Ernest Shackleton threatened to shoot the one sailor who was unwilling to support the goals of their quest for survival. Even though you won't shoot deserters or troublemakers, there will be times when you may need to underscore the serious nature of the quest's mission and demand the full commitment of your companions. Make sure you have your companions' full attention, commitment and passion early on, or else move quickly to replace them.

Share Information with Your Party Early and Often

During the quest's period of exploration, survival and successful completion will be issues to keep constantly in mind. The pathfinders must defer to those who can make a difference in the moment, regardless of rank, seniority or prior contributions. Therefore everyone needs to be kept in the loop. Your companions will expect to be active participants in information sharing and decision making on the journey. Sharing information and power and mutually assisting the companions is a hallmark of the quest leader.

To recap, your quest pathfinding teams must be passionate, lean and multifaceted. Find passionate companions, use specialists when needed, keep the team as small as possible, and use one another's expertise.

A good companion shortens the longest road.

— *Turkish proverb*

Questions for the Quest

1. What is your personal version of the call to adventure?
2. How will you share it with others?
3. How will you select the right companions?
4. What are your criteria for a great companion on the quest?
5. How will you keep your team swift and light?
6. What special expertise will you need? How will you get it?

6. Holdfasts

5. Path Finders

7. Instrument of Power

6. Holdfasts

People who make no mistakes lack boldness and the spirit of adventure. They are the brakes on the wheels of progress.

— Dr. Dale E. Turner, minister and author

Keep away from people who try to belittle your ambitions. Small people always do that, but the really great make you feel that you, too, can become great.

— Mark Twain, author and humorist

Before they can even dip their boats in the Missouri River, Lewis and Clark encounter an obstacle in the form of a person who was supposed to be a helper. There is only one boat builder able to create the most essential part of the journey's equipment: an iron-keeled longboat that will serve as the flagship of the flotilla. For weeks, the boat builder either shows up at work drunk or refuses to come in to work at all, causing the team to delay its start for more than a precious summer month.

Meet the Holdfast Forces

When you declare the call to adventure, you will attract others who possess the passion and expertise to help you drive the quest forward. Without the call, you could not assemble the companions for the quest. However, sounding the call will also arouse what Christopher Vogler calls holdfast forces in the organization.

Holdfast forces are people, circumstances and culture that protect the status quo. Holdfasts are activated by real or perceived risk. Many of these forces will be triggered by fear. These forces are afraid that your intent to lead your "corps of discovery" on an adventure into the unknown will upset the organization's status quo. In this, they are absolutely right.

Holding fast to the present produces at least a modicum of stability, equilibrium and promise of prosperity. The quest threatens the status quo – something that people in the organization have worked hard to establish. The holdfast forces tell you, "We have too much to lose to take such a chance." But to stick to "the proven path" now seems antithetical to you. Your response to the holdfasts is, "The status quo is broken; we can't stay here."

When you set out on your journey into the unknown, the foundations of the organization may shift, leaving holdfasts on shaky ground. They move to impede your progress. Every quest must face these forces.

Holdfasts, as individuals, keep a tight grip on the existing situation because they are getting some benefit from it. They may want to hold onto the powers that the organization presently possesses or that they possess within the organization. They may hang onto information and authority that gives them power. They can keep you stuck at home base and can block the quest for years. You cannot ignore the opposition of holdfast forces – make a plan to escape their hold and launch the quest.

Build political constituency for your quest early and nurture it over time. Jefferson spent years planning and building support in Congress for the Lewis and Clark Expedition. Columbus spent years petitioning the court of Queen Isabella. While you may not have years, plan to expend considerable energy building support for your quest and overcoming the holdfast forces.

Resistance can come in many forms:
- Restrictive policies and procedures
- Performance-management and incentive systems rewarding conforming behaviors
- Resource allocation that blocks resources from joining the quest
- Organizational structures that lock would-be adventurers within the existing roles and responsibilities
- Outright opposition from powerful people who don't believe in or support the call to adventure
- So-called supporters blocking you from what they see as an ill-conceived, risky venture

Overcome Exasperation

Most of us find it frustrating and exhausting to deal with the holdfast forces. Yet for all the exasperation they cause, they also serve some positive purpose. Holdfast forces keep the organization from giving up something that has been dearly gained just to pursue a new quest. It is a test of wills: the holdfast forces vs. the call to adventure. If the holdfast forces are stronger than the call to adventure, then the quest will be halted or delayed. If the call is stronger, then the pathfinders will eventually overcome those forces. A great number of bold leaders and pathfinders, from Jefferson (with his protégé Lewis) to South African anti-apartheid leader

Nelson Mandela and labor activist Erin Brockovich, were blocked for years before they finally overcame the holdfasts, thereby proving their readiness to launch the journeys.

Break Away!

If you could operate within the normal bounds and constraints set by the organization, then holdfast forces would be less of an issue. But quests do not unfold at home base. They happen beyond the threshold of discovery. Every successful quest had to break away from home base – or else be thwarted by holdfast forces.

Quests do not play out at home base, because home base is the place where the models of reality are known and agreed upon, not where breakthroughs are discovered. Any quest must unfold in the uncharted territory: in the realm of the undiscovered. Leaving home base creates freedom from the constraints of the organization's policies, methods and culture.

Many pathfinder teams choose to run under the radar to escape the holdfast forces. These are the skunk-works teams that create breakthroughs in spite of the constraints of the organization. I worked with one such group of people who called themselves The Underground. They thought of themselves as true heroes and made every effort to rise above the constraints of home base. I've worked with other teams that moved to a green-field setting to break free.

Another strategy, described by Gordon MacKenzie, author of *Orbiting the Giant Hairball*, described home base as an organizational "hairball" that will entangle and entrap those who seek to discover and innovate. In his conception of home base, only those who break free of the dragging gravity of the hairball remain free to pursue the quest. Now is the time to free yourself from the daily entanglements of business-as-usual methods and fully engage in the quest.

Watch Out for Overprotective People

Surprisingly, much of the resistance to the quest comes from seemingly well-intentioned supporters who are attempting to protect you from harm, to save you from yourself and what they see as your harebrained ideas. These well-wishers may support the call to adventure superficially, but they may not see the need to pursue the quest beyond home base, away from the conventional support of the organization, in the risky unknown territory of discovery and innovation. Unfortunately, in trying to provide conventional ways of support, they can actually serve to lock you and your fellow pathfinders into the status quo.

A manager from a communications technology group offered to help a pathfinder team address the challenge of instantaneous communication on nursing units. The manager offered to allow the team to pilot a new wireless telephone technology. She offered to provide equipment and training within eighteen months to support the team. However, the team needed a solution within a few weeks. (Remember, since quests are undertaken to relieve suffering in the organization, quests are time-urgent). The team could not use a solution that was even eighteen weeks away. When the team tried to bring in a temporary cellular solution to meet their goals, the technology manager resisted the team's efforts, even though cell phones had been approved for use in the hospital. She wanted to protect the hospital from a one-time use of technology that might later delay the ultimate solution.

Programs can be Holdfast Forces

Proven-path programs can themselves become holdfast forces. Watch out for those who do not want to send you off on your quest until you have completed a wall-to-wall improvement program, such as Six Sigma, change acceleration programs, and leadership effectiveness training. The company may have invested a lot of resources and money in such a program and, if the program's aims seem at all similar to your quest, you will face a holdfast situation. Since the steps of these programs are already known and understood, you have a clue that the program is not going on your quest.

Why can't your pathfinder team work within the existing methodology and demonstrate the effectiveness of these change programs to the organization? Because programmatic change is antithetical to the quest.

In fact, I've seen pathfinder teams co-opted by Six Sigma programs, forced through time-consuming training, assigned blackbelt advisors, and forced to formulate their quest as a problem that was amenable to solution with Six Sigma methods. While Six Sigma tools may be useful to the pathfinders, being sucked into the gravity field of a Six Sigma program, or any other wall-to-wall program, will firmly lock your pathfinder team down at home base and kill your quest.

Quest teams live off the land in the wilderness. Lewis and Clark did not bring enough elk meat with them to feed about thirty workers for three years; instead, they ate what they found on the way. Likewise, you and your pathfinder team should not overload yourselves with cumbersome organizational programs whose need for compliance will slow down progress on your quest.

While it's true that holdfast forces are an obstacle to the quest, they also serve a beneficial purpose. They test the readiness of the leaders and their pathfinders to undertake the journey. If the holdfasts overcome the pathfinders, they will be saved from a potentially disastrous journey for which they were not fully prepared. However, if your pathfinder team prevails, then you will have proven yourselves ready to launch. You will also build valuable capability through the struggle with the holdfast forces that will serve you well on your journey. The holdfast forces may also keep you from launching the quest prematurely.

Mature Organizations Breed Strong Holdfast Forces

However, if holdfast forces are exceptionally strong, as is often the case in mature organizations, then no would-be quest may ever be able to break free of their hold, even when the pathfinders are abundantly prepared. When holdfast forces are too strong and entrenched, they will stifle the propensity to quest.

Killing all quests – a common problem in mature organizations – will have disastrous consequences for the organization. Without the benefits a quest provides, the organization will inevitably stagnate, decline, lose vitality, and ultimately surrender to collapse or absorption.

Breaking free of the holdfast forces is your first survival imperative. You must free your team from holdfasts if you expect to complete your quest to discover future sources of vitality.

Build Political Support

Committed pathfinders and their sponsors need to use every means at their disposal to overcome holdfast forces. In general, two conditions must be met to overcome the holdfasts:

1. You will need to envision a compelling image of how things will be after the quest.
2. You will need political constituency to back that model.

You will need to engage the holdfasts, strengthening your call to adventure or modifying the goals of the quest to contain the needs of the holdfasts. Just having a better model will not be sufficient. As Ralph Stacey pointed out in "Managing the Unknowable," building political constituency is an essential skill for the sponsors of the quest.

Sponsors use, to great effect, the political tools of persuasion, negotiation, and discussion to spread or amplify new ideas throughout the organization. A small change, in the form of a new issue dimly perceived by one or two managers, can escalate into the undertaking of a major new activity by the company.

If you have no sponsor to help you build political support, you will want to cultivate one before going further. The sponsor needs to have the clout to:

- Attract or provide resources for the quest.
- Connect the quest pathfinders with those who can sanction the quest.
- Promote the quest at high levels in the organization.
- Clearly articulate the call to adventure to others in the organization.

You may find that those in the organization who are absorbed in programmatic change — for example, culture change or Lean Principles — may protest that the pathfinders are receiving attention and resources for which they themselves have been clamoring. They will point out the unfairness of this and prophesy that their own programs will be put at risk.

At this point, the sponsor must make the case that the quest itself, while not a programmatic method, is a systematic means to discover a breakthrough. After all, you are not trying to fix what is under the bell-shaped curve: improve performance or restore stability. You are shooting for a breakthrough result, an outlier, far from the mean. You are trying to discover the seeds for a higher-order system, a new way of functioning.

Let Your Sponsor Intervene

I mentioned that the sponsor can intervene to defend the quest and the pathfinders from the holdfast forces. Sponsors have some advantages over the pathfinders when it comes to holding the holdfast forces at bay. They often have more power, influence, and authority than the pathfinders, and they often operate at the same or higher level in the organization than the holdfasts. If you need protection, call on the sponsor to intervene. If they believe in the quest, they will support and defend you.

When Meriwether Lewis needed funds to get the iron-keeled boat built, he had Jefferson, the greatest sponsor at that propitious time in American history. For his journey, Lewis had carte blanche, a letter of approval from his president advising all those whom Lewis met on his journey, even citizens of other countries, to give Lewis whatever he needed, and Jefferson would reimburse them.

Holdfast forces are usually not out to get you. They are not even bent on destroying the quest itself. They are out to protect the organization from risky ventures and probably help you save your career. You must make the case in your call to adventure that the quest is not only worthwhile, it is essential for everyone's survival.

Recognize holdfast forces are forces of stability and equilibrium. They promote a safe, proven path. Yours is a different path.

Most people have come to prefer certain of life's experiences and deny and reject others, unaware of the value of the hidden things that may come wrapped in plain and even ugly paper.... In rejecting change and risk, we often cheat ourselves of the quest; in denying our suffering, we may never know our strength or our greatness.

— Dr. Rachel Naomi Remen, clinical
professor of family and community medicine

Questions for the Quest

1. Who are the actual or potential holdfasts you face in your quest?
2. What non-human holdfast forces do you face?
3. How will the call to adventure help you break free?
4. Where can you build political support? How will you do it?
5. How will you engage the executive sponsor of the quest?
6. Has your organization sanctioned quests of any kind? If not, how will you break that barrier?
7. What are the consequences of losing a political struggle to launch the quest?
8. Why is the quest worth the struggle?

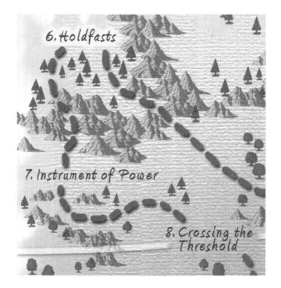

7. Instrument of Power

Behold the sword of power! Excalibur! Forged when the world
was young.

— Merlin, wizard in King Arthur tales

For Meriwether Lewis to make a journey across America, time was at a premium. The winter of 1803-04 was fast approaching. President Jefferson waited anxiously for the trip to begin, while Lewis spent precious weeks studying under some of the nation's leading scientists and doctors, acquiring knowledge needed to complete the mission. As summer turned to autumn, Lewis overspent his budget, buying the best weaponry the world had to offer, including the Philadelphia rifle. He also bought the best scientific instruments, including the Chronometer, an exorbitant item on the budget but necessary to determine latitude.

Choose Your Instrument of Power

As Lewis knew, it would have been organizational suicide to embark on such a crucial journey without proper knowledge and equipment. Myth and legend captured this truth in stories about the hero acquiring the instrument of power: a magic amulet, a special sword, a cloak of invisibility, and so on. For Luke Skywalker, his Jedi lightsaber and his initial Jedi training under Obi Wan Kenobi were essential to his quest.

You will need to acquire new tools that will prove essential to the success of your quest. While an organizational quest rarely crosses physical territory, the team needs its instruments of power as well, for its quest crosses uncharted territory of another kind. The territory of the quest is not the same as home base. Tools that work at home base may not necessarily serve you once you have set off on your expedition.

Instruments of power allow pathfinders to survive the uncharted territory of systems, strategy, and markets, where discoveries abound and rapid innovation is a necessity. For Lewis, his instruments of power helped him discover more about celestial navigation, medicine, botany, zoology, fossils, and cartography. For you, it might be tools to understand customers, formulate new strategy, reinvent processes, conceptualize new systems, or make the most of new technologies. Is there some new knowledge or skill that you will need to increase your chances of success? Those are your instruments of power, and they will amplify your capability on the quest.

On many of the organizational quests I have facilitated, pathfinder teams have found certain tools to be enormously useful for their cause. I worked with an emergency services team of pathfinders that acquired tools for complex computer simulation of emergency department operations.

On another quest, an airport customer-experience pathfinder team learned to use the Critical Incident Technique, a powerful tool for uncovering hidden customer expectations. A team in a large information technology company became knowledgeable in lean operating principles. A pathfinder team in an insurance company applied neural networks and genetic algorithms while on their quest.

What Tools will Amplify Your Power?

Knowing which tool will serve your mission is a matter of fit. What tools will amplify your power? What tools will improve your chances of successful completion? What tools will help you make sense of the new information that you will encounter? Choose tools with practical application to the challenges you will likely face, for example, systems-thinking tools may be a better fit than failure-mode-and-effects analysis. Like choosing survival gear, go for the few select tools that will amplify your power and allow you to travel light.

If you have a mentor, use the mentor's experience and expertise to help you identify what instruments of power will be useful. Mentors have been on similar journeys and will know, in part, what you can expect.

Choose Tools Quickly but Wisely

Besides finding out which tools to use, you will have to acquire the tools relatively quickly. Lewis could only spend two months with the some of the nation's leading scientists. With so little time, he had to put in "hard, intensive study in a variety of disciplines under severe time pressure." You won't have time to earn a degree in whole-system design before launching your quest. You must quickly identify what you will need for your quest. The inclination to master entire methodologies (such as team dynamics and organizational communication) is merely a holdfast force. Don't confuse that in-clination with your real need to acquire just the necessary survival tools. Competence, not expertise, is needed to launch the journey.

Since you don't have to learn entire methodologies, just acquire the parts you believe you will use. Once the quest is upon you (which began when you sounded the call to adventure), the wheel of time is turning. Breaking free of ties at home base is now prior-ity one. When Lewis' trip to Philadelphia was delayed, he had to cut his education short; the launch could not be delayed.

While it's true you will need to acquire new tools quickly, sim-ply skipping this stage and launching the quest without survival tools will put the quest in jeopardy. Consider Captain William Edward Parry's failure to learn sled dog handling techniques. It led to his death and the deaths of the entire party on his ill-fated Antarctic quest. Acquiring the right tools can make the difference between success and failure.

Are there tools that every pathfinder should learn? I used to believe in a list of basic tools that would help every team.

However, I've observed many successful organizational quests without the use of such tools, and I now believe that there is no top-ten list of survival tools. So I've shortened my list to just one tool: running trials and experiments. All pathfinders will encounter a road of trials where they must make sense of novel situations, for-mulate hypotheses, try something different, evaluate the results, and then decide what to do next. This is how they build new capability and, eventually, achieve a breakthrough. Knowing how to run a trial or experiment is the prime skill. It is essential for success.

Do You Need Specialized Tools?

There may be good reasons to go beyond your organization's own inventory of possible survival tools. Like Lewis, you may need to look outside your own type of organization and acquire the best tools on the planet. You may need to learn from the leading experts of the day in science, engineering, medicine, and other disciplines. I recall a client who needed to understand the principles of a high-reliability organization such as an aircraft carrier or nuclear power plant; they contacted one of the two professors who wrote the book on the subject and developed expertise to use principles on their quest for dramatically fewer errors and failures. Another team contacted a world-recognized expert on the Theory of Inventive Problem Solving to help reduce the occurrences of retained sponges after surgery. When feasible, acquire survival tools from leading experts outside your organization.

> A nurse on a hospital-capacity quest had written her master's thesis on methods for evaluating emergency room patients before they were moved to a nursing unit. During the quest, she used her expertise to help the pathfinders design a new admitting process for emergency room patients. Her contribution was a significant part of a breakthrough in hospital throughput.

The Tool is Not the Quest Itself

When acquiring such tools, be careful not mistake the tools for the object of your organizational quest. There are people in every mature organization who have confused tools with the quest itself. For example, some believe that adopting Six Sigma quality from wall to wall is, in and of itself, a worthy organizational change strategy.

While it may be admirable to provide everyone with such tools, it is not a substitute for the quest. Six Sigma, for example, may provide tools for the pathfinders, giving them a means to improve their odds on the quest, but Six Sigma itself is rarely the object of their quest. The right tools make the pathfinders more powerful, helping them navigate new territory and achieve the breakthroughs they need to create new sources of organizational vitality, but they are not the reason for the quest.

Survival tools give pathfinder teams new capabilities, but that is rarely sufficient to successfully fulfill the quest. On the journey, your team must build new capabilities as you overcome obstacles and complete trials. Since the path of the quest is relatively unknown, you cannot prepare for all contingencies in advance. You must also rely on new information discovered on the quest, relying on new tools acquired or constructed as they progress. Therefore, the best survival tools are those that give the pathfinders added resilience during the quest – tools that help you create what you need to survive as the journey unfolds.

The best pathfinders figure out what tools are needed and quickly acquire the tools and training, often from the experts. They avoid getting trapped by the methodologies that are often wrapped around the tools. They encourage team members to acquire specialized tools, and they add subject matter experts to the team when necessary, so long as the experts can also participate as full team members.

Questions for the Quest

1. What tools or techniques do you need to complete your quest?
2. How will those tools make your team more effective?
3. How can you use tools to lower your risk?
4. If you only have time to acquire a few tools, what would they be?

5. Who on the team should learn to use certain tools?
6. Where and how can you acquire these tools and skills quickly?
7. What specialists must you have on your team?

Threshold of Discovery

Discovery

Phase Two: Exploration

Now is the time to move out into the exploration portion of your quest. Your path of exploration will take you into unmapped territory where unexpected discoveries and big breakthroughs are possible. If you can enter this phase without preconceived solutions, you can discover, innovate and build vital capability. You will face significant challenges, but you will also meet helpers and allies. If you can learn and develop enough within the time constraints, you will face the ultimate test, the last obstacle between you and the big breakthrough.

Crossing the Threshold

The threshold is a literal or figurative boundary that marks the limits of the common, everyday world. Beyond this frontier boundary is uncharted territory — a realm of discovery. In organizations the threshold is constructed from shared culture, shared mental models, ways of working, policies, and so on. Upon crossing the threshold, pathfinders move from the business-as-usual world into uncharted territory, where they begin the process of exploration and discovery.

Orienteering

After crossing the threshold, pathfinders must quickly orient themselves and gain traction in this new territory. They have to discover basic laws that govern there and orient themselves toward their ultimate goal. Here they explore the situation, begin identifying new ideas, and prepare to move forward with experiments. Regardless how adept they were with the old ways, they might not comprehend the new territory's laws or might fail to challenge long-held assumptions.

Helpers and Allies

By sounding the call to adventure, leaders make themselves available to all types of helpers in their environment. The mentor is the initial helper, but once the pathfinders cross the threshold of adventure, other helpers and allies appear, often unexpectedly, to offer assistance and support. Helpers and allies can offer technical assistance, subject matter expertise, encouragement and support, political support, or anything else that can move the pathfinders forward in their journey. Pathfinders also seek out helpers and allies as they run into challenges, obstacles and opportunities.

Path of Trials

The path of the trials presents challenges to the pathfinders. The challenges generally present themselves as a series of tests increasing in difficulty. In organizational quests, pathfinders typically create trials themselves as they test the feasibility of innovative ideas. Each trial may be more challenging than the last, as the pathfinders grow in confidence and capability. The pathfinders discover, gather information, and attempt more challenging trials. The pathfinders overcome unforeseen obstacles and setbacks along the path.

The trials amplify their capability to the point that they can face the ultimate test, try the big change, and achieve the breakthrough.

Ultimate Test

The ultimate test is the great challenge or obstacle at the nadir, zenith, or far edge of the journey. It is the supreme ordeal that blocks the final move to the breakthrough. Failing to pass the ultimate test will cause the quest to fail. Then again, successfully meeting the challenge of the ultimate test sets the pathfinders up to attempt the big breakthrough. Completing the ultimate test takes the pathfinders to a point of realization and greater understanding that allows them to mount the final assault on their goal. Often the ultimate test requires that the pathfinders face some metaphorical death that forces them to let go of the last vestige of outmoded assumptions that are holding them back from the breakthrough.

8. Crossing the Threshold

One does not discover new lands without consenting to lose sight of the shore for a very long time.

— Andre Gide, winner of Nobel Prize in literature

Until one is committed, there is hesitancy, the chance to draw back, always ineffectiveness.

— W.H. Murray, Scottish mountain climber

The Lewis and Clark Expedition enters the threshold zone when they set off from Camp Dubois in the big iron keelboat and two smaller boats. They proceed up the Missouri by rowing, sailing, using setting poles, and sometimes wading along the bank to haul the boats upriver. Five weeks later, the expedition passes La Charette, a cluster of seven dwellings. They are still less than sixty miles up the Missouri. This will be the last group of European settlers the expedition will see on this river. The Corps leaves behind the last vestiges of a familiar world and continues up the Lower Missouri River, crossing into unfamiliar territory. This is the Expedition's threshold of discovery.

Thresholds Mark the Divide

Throughout the millennia, in stories both true and imagined, the threshold is typically represented as a great physical divide. The threshold can be anything that separates the known from the unknown world: a body of water, a mountain range, a desert, or a mysterious doorway.

In the movie "The Wizard of Oz," Dorothy's threshold between her tornado-tossed house and the land beyond the rainbow was clearly delineated by a change from black and white to color film. Luke Skywalker and Ben Kenobi began their threshold crossing at the spaceport where Han Solo launched them on a dangerous ride into hyperspace. The Lewis and Clark Expedition navigated up the Missouri and soon crossed into *terra incognito*.

The crossing from the common world to a special world can often be mapped in a geographical movement, as in the Age of Discovery or in the Space Race. But quests can unfold in other ways, as well.

The idea of crossing a threshold into an unknown realm is more difficult to take in for organizational adventurers. In organizations, the demarcation between our normal world and the realm of adventure (where the action is) is often abstract and blurred. Thresholds do not have to be physical. For example, when some organization refuses to approve a proposal for a breakthrough initiative, it may be, in effect, saying that the initiative is beyond the boundary of normal practice. By disapproving, it is holding back the perceived chaos of a disruptive initiative, keeping it from undermining the stability of the organization.

Sometimes pathfinder teams actually do relocate physically to a green-field location or to a project center, where the environment feels physically different. More often, the team meets in familiar surroundings. In those cases, the unknown territory represents new topics of exploration, new principles, and new trials to be pursued by the team. Whether in the physical world or the world of ideas, the threshold is real and presents risks as well as opportunities.

The stakes are high. Failing to cross the threshold will terminate the quest. The preparation will be wasted. The call to adventure will be postponed and the companions will disband. At the least, if the threshold crossing fails, the adventure will degrade into a pedestrian undertaking.

Cross to a Different World

The threshold of discovery is a literal or figurative boundary marking the limits of the everyday world. Beyond this boundary is uncharted territory. The threshold of discovery demarcates the common world from the larger, unknown realm of discovery.

The common world is bounded by what is known and what is agreed upon. It is constructed from the shared culture, shared mental models, common systems, ways of working and so on. Conversely, the realm of discovery is marked by unexplored territory, unknown laws and principles, unfamiliar ways of being, and the raw material of new paradigms. Possibilities for breakthroughs are plentiful.

Crossing the threshold is not mandatory. Not every problem calls for a breakthrough. If we choose to work with familiar knowledge and opinions and if we can live with business-as-usual solutions, then we don't need to cross the threshold. We only make the crossing because we need to explore and discover, build new capabilities, achieve breakthroughs that are only available when we work with novelty. Cross the threshold only if you need breakthroughs.

In addition to acting as a boundary, the threshold of discovery is also the perimeter of a container. It keeps the systems of the everyday world from drifting away from equilibrium, destabilizing and collapsing into chaos. The threshold is the perimeter that contains the everyday, business-as-usual world.

The threshold confines the resources of the common world, keeping those resources from leaking away into random pursuits that do not contribute to the stability of the organization. When the organization disapproves an initiative, it conserves its resources for other uses. Mature organizations tend to confine their resources, sometimes permanently, unless the need is very great. If you want to quest beyond the threshold, your call to adventure and your preparation must transcend this organizational inclination.

The threshold also marks the beginning of active transformation, a prelude to a new beginning. The threshold is a transitory area, a portal to another realm. As pathfinders enter the threshold area, they begin to adjust to what lies beyond. They are now fully engaged in the adventure.

Traversing the Threshold Zone

Crossing the threshold is not a business-as-usual undertaking. A casual approach is unwise. Casual teams will fail to realize that the proven path ends abruptly at the threshold of discovery. They will simply miss the fact that something significant has changed, that the assumptions of the everyday world cannot be assumed to hold.

I have worked with teams of pathfinders who believed they were still on the proven path, engaged in the comfortable process of incremental change. They pulled out the process maps and project plans and were ready to search for fail points in the existing system. Pathfinders must be bold, lest they be seduced by the promise of the proven path.

Marking the Threshold Crossing

Consider kicking off the crossing with an intense experience such as a field trip, retreat or other event. Visit other innovative companies, attend an energizing conference, or plan an adventure-based team building experience. Team members may question the need for such full commitment, but it is a great way to break away from business as usual and feel the change in state of moving onto the quest. Use the threshold crossing to create commitment and then don't look back.

Remind the pathfinders of their call to adventure. If it seems too weak, strengthen it now. Use the call to connect; the team is connected to the prize being sought and the tremendous rewards for a successful quest.

> A healthcare CEO told his organization that the prize he sought was a fully integrated healthcare system. The prize was nothing less than delivering the next generation of healthcare. Community members who suffered from lack of access to healthcare would benefit tremendously from seamless care. It was clear to everyone why crossing the threshold and committing to the quest was so important to his organization. The organization responded to the challenge.

Sometimes would-be pathfinders cross false thresholds. Teams believe that they are moving into or beyond the threshold zone when, in fact, they are still operating well within the sphere of their everyday world. It's easy to be fooled by sense of movement toward a goal. Under these conditions, leaders can confuse basic change-management practices with the quest.

Pursuing routine change rarely takes the organization beyond the threshold. Remember that most organizational improvement is intended to restore or strengthen equilibrium and uses business-as-usual approaches. It does not take the group near the threshold. I worked with a team in an insurance company that would wisely take time to pause and ask themselves, "Are we still moving toward breakthrough?"

Like the portals in myth and science fiction, the door of opportunity might not remain open long. The decision to cross is often time-critical. The team must get "unstuck" from home territory and move rapidly into uncharted territory. Don't let your team get bogged down at the threshold. Set a tone of time urgency and push for a prompt crossing. Priorities change, budgets are revised, and leaders come and go. Commit the organization fully to the quest while it possesses the will to work for transformation. Move quickly across the threshold.

Threshold Ceremony

On Independence Day, July 4, 1804, exactly one year after Jefferson announced the Louisiana Purchase, the Corps of Discovery celebrated their first Independence Day west of the Mississippi. They fired the keelboat's cannon, drank an extra ration of whiskey, and named a nearby creek Independence Creek. This was the Expedition's threshold ceremony, marking their penetration of the zone between their home world and the unknown territory of the Great Plains.

Ceremonies after the threshold crossing are common in the stories of exploration and the legends of heroes. Their thresholds were physical as well as physiological barriers. The celebration marked an important crossing. On the other hand, thresholds in organizations tend to be intangible. They can be obscured in the crush of daily activity.

Crossing the threshold may seem superficial, no more than a mere change of subject, just another team meeting. That's why it is important to mark the threshold crossing with a ceremony. The threshold ceremony is the organizational equivalent to celebrations that send off modern cruise ships. It marks the crossing out of the everyday world and signals that the travelers won't be looking back.

It is a time for neither looking back nor looking too far forward. Use the threshold ceremony as a means of focusing the pathfinder team's attention on the crossing.

No matter how you choose to celebrate the crossing, use the threshold ceremony to make it clear that things will now be very different from the business-as-usual world the team is leaving. Without a threshold ceremony, the team risks drifting back into business as usual and losing the opportunity to quest at all.

Threshold Guardians

Every quest is full of challenges. Often the first challenge to be met head-on is a huge obstacle embodied in the threshold guardian. Guardians of thresholds can be merciless and may cut down anyone who isn't committed to decisive action. This is the first major test of nerve and resolve on the team.

Lewis and Clark meet three threshold guardians in their crossing into uncharted territory. They first encounter a small delegation of Oto and Missouri Indians and are allowed passage. Next the Expedition holds friendly council with Yankton Sioux (near what is now Yankton, South Dakota). However, their encounter with the third guardian nearly ends in disaster. In September, near what is now Pierre, South Dakota, the Teton Sioux demand one of the boats as a payment for moving upriver.

The Teton Sioux are powerful and considered unfriendly by other tribes. Moreover, they can easily block further passage up the Missouri River. A fight nearly develops, but the diplomacy of a chief named Black Buffalo eventually defuses the predicament. For three more anxious days, the Expedition stays with the tribe, fearing all the while for their safety. It takes every ounce of Lewis and Clark's courage, restraint and diplomacy to gain passage and avert an early end to the Expedition.

Threshold guardians make their stand at the crossing point. Think of Jason and the Argonauts facing the Clashing Rocks at the narrow passage to the unknown sea. Or recall the Wicked Witch of the West blocking Dorothy's path just as she prepares to follow the yellow brick road.

In business, think of the executive who keeps demanding postponement of the launch until more is known and understood, clarified and cross-checked. Not every crossing results in an encounter with a threshold guardian, but you will want be prepared.

The guardian blocking the threshold is also associated with the idea of the hero falling into an abyss. Consider the influential Institute of Medicine report, "Crossing the Quality Chasm: A New Health System for the 21st Century."

While sounding a powerful call to adventure, it also clearly lays out the stakes for failing to go beyond business-as-usual methods and falling into the chasm, instead of making the transformational crossing. If you fall into the chasm, you will not be able to cross the threshold of discovery. You will be deflected back to everyday solutions, blocked from the quest.

I recall meeting with the leadership team of a regional hospital corporation. The team members described their recent misadventure this way: "We attempted to jump the curve to a radically different reimbursement model and instead fell into the abyss."

Their quest was blocked, and it took several years before they could mount another attempt.

Guardians serve a useful and important role. They keep the uncommitted and unprepared from crossing the threshold of discovery and running into disaster. Overcoming those guardians is often the first of many tests and trials on the adventure.

Make sure you find out who or what is blocking the quest (often behind the scenes), and either confront or circumvent the source. You cannot achieve dramatic success without negotiating entry into the unknown realm.

I worked with an emergency department team that had just launched its quest, when executive management abruptly demanded that they start using traditional (company-sanctioned) project management practices. The management wanted the pathfinders to report the team's plans, goals, and progress in detail every week. These guardians, seeking home-base controls, would have certainly killed the quest, had the sponsor not rallied to its defense. The team proceeded without home-base constraints and eventually achieved a breakthrough.

From This Point Forward, the Journey Has No Map

As pathfinders, you will need to make your own map. This begins by letting go of the first layer of preconceived assumptions about what is real and true and being open to new rules. You will need to press on through your uncertainties and anxieties about the uncharted journey ahead.

All pathfinding teams will find their own means of passage across the threshold zone. Jonah was pushed into action and given passage across the threshold by the whale. Columbus captained the Santa Maria beyond the known sea routes, while Lewis and Clark rowed up the Missouri River. How will you cross? Will you encourage a skunkworks? Will you set up a green-field location, launch your team on an adventurous fact-finding trip, or meet in an exceptional place? Whatever the case, beware of trying to find a trodden path as you pass through the threshold zone.

In a Norwegian fairy tale, the hero comes to a crossroads with three signs. The first sign says, "He who travels down this road will return unharmed." The second sign says, "He who travels this path may or may not return." The third sign says, "He who travels here will never return." The hero, without hesitation, chooses the third road. He crosses the threshold, stepping onto the most original path in search of his fortune.

Storyteller Laura Simms, in retelling this tale, points out that pathfinding heroes kill the safe path, doing away with their own limited vehicle of travel. This opens them to new worlds. How else will they discover the object of their quest? The invisible world, that world beyond the threshold, is real and will be ever-nourishing.

The hero will return, yes, but never to be the same again, bringing back the secret treasure of new awareness, which is priceless. Stepping beyond the threshold is a new way of seeing, an awakening. The journey begins at the crossing.

Questions for the Quest

1. Where have your organization's former frontiers been pushed out?
2. What marks the current threshold of discovery?
3. What obstacles or guardians block you?
4. How will you speed your passage?
5. How will you know that you have crossed into uncharted territory?

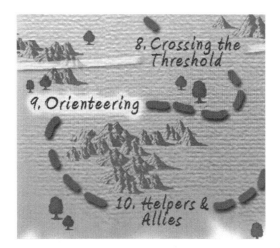

9. Orienteering

To be on the quest is nothing less than to become an asker of questions.

> — Sam Keen, author, professor and philosopher

Learning is not compulsory ... neither is survival.

> — W. Edwards Deming, father of the
> quality movement and industrial revival

In September 1804, the Lewis and Clark expedition moves into the Great Plains. This is clearly uncharted territory, with the party finding geography, plants and animals that are unknown in the East. For the first time, they see mule deer, coyotes, prairie dogs, and antelope. Lewis and Clark will eventually record 122 animals and 178 plants not scientifically recorded before.

Here is Territory Unlike Anything Else

Emerging from the threshold into terra incognito may well be a relief: "We did it," your team might want to say; "we made it beyond the threshold and past the threshold guardians!" True, your team has reached a territory unlike anything else that has been described before. Here are wonders waiting — expecting — to be explored.

Yet we all know that just beyond the threshold, adventurers instantly expose themselves to risk. In *The Lion, the Witch and the Wardrobe,* Lucy has just passed through her wardrobe threshold. But she is not inside the lovely snowy woods of Narnia five minutes before hearing tales about the White Witch. Just so, it may be that your pathfinder team may find new threats to discovery just beyond the crossing.

These stories tell us that this is not the time to let down your guard or be complacent. Yes, your pathfinder team achieved its first goal – to cross the threshold – but you have put yourselves in a dicey situation, attempting to make your way through uncharted territory with limited information.

Staying at Fort Mandan for as short a time as possible before taking off in the spring, Lewis and Clark made orienteering their top priority, learning everything they could about the territory they were about to enter. They received guidance from native tribes about how to travel the wilderness they were to cross. They hired interpreters who could help them communicate and trade with tribes further upriver.

Move Beyond the Threshold

The territory your pathfinder team has just entered presents a broad vista of new concepts, and opportunities — all of them beckoning to you. Standing in this unfamiliar place beyond the threshold, you want to know, "Now what?" Since you needed to abandon the proven-path approach so you could move beyond home base, the answer may not be obvious.

The short answer is, "Move out."

As soon as possible, get your bearings and start figuring out how to carry on in the new territory. Distance yourselves from the threshold. The idea of orienteering is to quickly assess the new terrain, get your bearings, set up navigation, then set out to find the prize.

The orienteering stage is when your pathfinder team quickly learns basic laws that govern the territory. Regardless how adept you were with the old ways, you may not comprehend the new territory's laws just yet. In fact, long-held assumptions will probably distort your perceptions. As you adjust to the new situation, you can head out, beginning to apply new principles. You will soon be using observations, experiments, and trials to confirm or refute your theories.

Once beyond the threshold zone, the journey begins in earnest, because your quest has crossed into territory where discovery and innovation abound. Insist that your pathfinder team operate away from the organizational comfort zone, where the lure to return to home base is strongest. Field trips take the team away from the literal home base of the office or store, opening up your team to new ideas, new ways of solving challenges.

Beware of Bending the Map

When people become lost in the forest, it is often because they have wandered into unfamiliar territory that they thought was a familiar path. The problem is not that they are standing on new ground but that they believe it to be old ground. Many who perish actually "bend the map." They mentally force the map they have to fit their current position, even though the map actually depicts a different area. Thus their map becomes a danger rather than a benefit, leading them in the wrong direction.

Bending the map is also a danger for your pathfinding team. Here, bending the map means applying principles from the business-as-usual world to the new territory, even though they no longer apply. Not only are old principles misleading, but they also discourage your team from discovering new principles.

For an information-technology client of mine, high staff utilization was believed to reduce costs and deliver systems to customers more quickly. This belief in utilization was a hindrance when the pathfinder teams wanted to experiment with the principles of flow — rapid cycle time, fast turnover, and buffers to synchronize processes. They clung to the idea that high utilization was good in spite of the emerging evidence — they were bending the map. Part of orienteering is making sure that you are not using the wrong maps, even if it means using no map at all.

Get Your Bearings

Do not rely on existing maps. They can provide a general outline of the new territory but will not be sufficient to blaze new paths. Lewis and Clark obtained the best maps available before starting their expedition, but Clark made his own detailed maps as he discovered the true nature of the territory. Others then used his maps for decades to follow.

This is the point where your pathfinding team must realize that it is time to make your own maps. No X marks the spot that locates the object of your quest. Neither the spot nor the path to get there will ever be the same for two pathfinding teams. No proven-path program will guide you there.

As Joseph Campbell said in *The Power of Myth,* "This path has no map. The traveler needs to discover the map or make his own. The Grail Knights entered the forest where the forest was darkest, and there was not a path." Like Lewis and Clark, you will have to make your own maps as you go, blazing your own trail. Orienteering is essential precisely because you must create your own path.

Orienteering activities for the organizational quest vary greatly from journey to journey. Each pathfinding team must remember its own objective (recalling its own call to adventure) and be mindful of the new rules that govern this puzzling territory. Here are some orienteering techniques that I have used with organizational teams:

1. Assess the current situation. Determine how your organization is performing today, and talk about what is needed for a breakthrough. Determine how other organizations perform today.

2. Determine compass measures. Quests are managed with a compass, not a precise stopwatch. Compass measures are those broad performance measures that tell the pathfinder team if it moving closer to its ultimate objective. Is patient length of stay decreasing? Is customer satisfaction going up? Is critical system availability increasing? Two to four (six at most) big-picture measures are enough to keep your team moving toward its goal.

3. Capture top-of-mind ideas. What ideas do the pathfinders and sponsors have right now that might move the team closer to its ultimate objective. Some of these ideas, while

not complete, can guide your pathfinding team to its first trials. For example, an idea for a novel use of physicians, taken from another hospital, led eventually to a breakthrough in length of stay, which coincidentally, did not ultimately use physicians. Capture top-of-mind ideas. They may prefigure the key to the final solution.

4. Understand expectations of the stakeholders back at home base. What outcome is desired? How will your path move you toward meeting those expectations? Check to make sure that you are clear about your objective, or you could find yourself on the wrong quest. Be clear about your call to adventure. Frequently pause to research customer expectations before you fully answer these questions. For example, one quest team's research uncovered that business banking customers valued in-depth support more than sophisticated financial products.

5. Identify the gap between where you are and where you need to be. Now that you are in new territory, it is time to reassess the gap that your quest must close. Will the quest require previously unanticipated time or resources? Are the actions you expected still appropriate? For example, some pathfinders working on clinical research quickly discovered that they would have to deploy new information systems that were not anticipated during the launch. Their project, expected to take only twelve weeks, would take more than a year to complete.

6. Recall past pathfinder work and innovative practices in related and unrelated industries. Have others traveled similar territory? What can you learn from their efforts? Do desk research, and ask around. Check with people in your orga-

nization who have tackled the same problem. For example, an airport discovered that a well-known hotel had dealt with a similar problem: how to achieve high customer satisfaction in a facility that was aging. The hotel's ideas led to new areas of exploration at the airport.

7. Conduct background research to gain familiarity with the subject. Are there critical technologies or techniques that the pathfinder team must understand? For example, pathfinders working on the reliability of clinical information systems determined that they could apply principles used in High Reliability Organizations, such as nuclear power plants and aircraft carrier flight decks.

8. Identify sources of useful information, including subject matter experts. Determine who has information and knowledge that you need, and contact them. Be aggressive in going outside your organization and outside your industry. Remember that if you work only with what you already know, you will not be able to achieve a breakthrough. Novel ideas are essential to a successful quest.

9. Estimate timing for milestones. Now that orienteering has given you a better sense of where you are and which direction to begin, you can identify milestones and estimate timing for reaching them. These are estimates, not commitments, since you have much to discover, so don't be trapped by traditional project-management approaches. Instead, use the milestones to reassess your next steps.

10. Enjoy the process of discovery. Acknowledge your accomplishments. You have the freedom to explore and create. This is the joy of the journey.

To the pathfinding team that wanted to eliminate delays and overcrowding in their emergency room, things seemed overwhelming at first. Physicians were openly skeptical of the effort. Process flow charts were complex and confusing. There was no obvious place to make a significant difference. Some team members were impatient, wanting to move immediately into implementing small changes.

Yet the team accepted the challenge of orienteering. They investigated practices at other hospitals, visiting several emergency rooms in other states. They helped construct a computer simulation to better understand the subtle workings of their emergency room. They created compass measures to guide the rest of the journey. The team members decided to focus on understanding the principles of rapid flow, quick turnaround and adjusting to peak demand. Their careful orienteering set them up for eventual breakthroughs.

While the Orienteering stage presents any number of learning opportunities, it is not a place to linger. Remember that the quest is a race against time across unknown territory. Do not wait until you feel fully prepared. Time is always of the essence — and always a scarce resource. Do not allow your team to get dragged down in detailed planning, contingency preparation, and second guessing. Move out as soon as you have what you need in order to navigate the next stage of your journey.

Leave the beaten track occasionally and dive into the woods. Every time you do so, you will be certain to find something that you have never seen before. Follow it up, explore all around it, and before you know it, you will have something worth thinking about to occupy your mind. All really big discoveries are the results of thought.

— *Alexander Graham Bell, inventor*

Questions for the Quest

1. What actions could help your team gain its bearings after crossing into uncharted territory?
2. What helpers could you contact?
3. What is unknown that you must attempt to understand immediately?
4. How can your team learn as much as possible about your organization's situation?
5. How can your team find the external leaders in your area of exploration?
6. What measures will become your compass? How will you dispense with traditional project management?
7. What untested assumptions are you bringing with you from home base? How will you challenge them?
8. How are you unconsciously bending the map to fit the new terrain?

10. Helpers and Allies

There is no more noble occupation in the world than to assist another human being, to help someone succeed.
— Alan Loy McGinnis, psychotherapist

Without their meticulous preparation for the Expedition, Lewis and Clark would have failed in their quest. Yet even with their commendable preparations, the Corps would almost certainly have met a much different fate if they had not met helpers on the journey.

In October 1804, the Corps of Discovery arrives at the extensive earth-lodge villages of the Mandan and Hidatsa people. Since it is already late in the season, the captains decide to winter here, and the Corps builds Fort Mandan across the river from the main village. Here they meet their two main helpers of the journey: Toussaint Charbonneau, a French Canadian fur trader living among the Hidatsa, and his young Shoshone wife, Sacagawea. Sacagawea had been captured by the Hidatsa several years earlier and was eventually sold to Charbonneau. Both can translate several languages, including Indian dialects, and both know the customs of some of the tribes upriver.

As far as Lewis and Clark know, no one with equivalent skills exists in the United States. If they had required such skills before launching, the Expedition might well have stalled before even reaching the threshold of their quest. Like many adventurers, they set out without knowing exactly who they would meet on their journey, deciding to rely on the opportunity to meet helpers on the way.

One of Charbonneau's two wives will stay home, but Sacagawea expresses great interest in accompanying Charbonneau and the Corps on the journey, to see the Pacific Ocean. Later, Sacagawea will come to the rescue of the Corps on several key occasions. She saves Clark's journals when the boat overturns in rapids. She guides the Corps to the headwaters of the Missouri and the home of the Shoshone Indians, the first tribe they encounter after leaving Fort Mandan. In August 1805, Sacagawea is asked to translate in negotiations with the Shoshone Indian chief for desperately needed horses. Remarkably, the Shoshone chief, Cameahwait, turns out to be the brother of Sacagawea, and after a tearful reunion, he provides the horses. Without the horses, the Corps could not have crossed into the next stage of their journey.

Helpers will Find You

More than likely, you will meet helpers on your quest who will be pivotal to your success. When you are open to helpers, resources will rush to meet you. Inevitably, some individual or organization you cannot anticipate will come to your aid and help you continue your quest.

During one night shift, a Dr. Howe, part of a pathfinding team, decided that he would try out some of the ideas that his hospital's team had been discussing. He put five patient charts under his arm and proceeded to the waiting room to try out the new rapid-care ideas that were part of the hospital team's ongoing quest. It was a breakthrough that led to a new method of patient care that eventually changed the industry. Without Dr. Howe as helper, the pathfinder team could have easily stalled.

Sacagawea and Dr. Howe are both examples of how life is generous to those who pursue their quest. When you need to move to the next step, helpers will appear. They often appear unexpectedly, marking a shift or new direction in the quest.

In Arthurian legends, these shifts were sometimes marked by a meeting with a hermit. A knight, exhausted and discouraged, would stumble upon a hermit's hut. The hermit would invite him in for a meal and a rest.

Of course, the knight received much more: with stories and encouragement, the hermit helped the questing knight in several ways. The hermit would give the knight food, refreshment and rest but also sage advice that unlocked the secret to the next stage of the quest. Reinvigorated, and a bit wiser, the knight would leave the hermit. Now he was armed with the insight required to start the next phase of his adventure.

Aiding your team in very similar ways on your organizational quest, helpers

- Explain the significance of events you encounter
- Provide reassurance; steady you if you are becoming uncertain
- Help you develop your skills
- Transmit profound knowledge you need
- Help if you have lost your way and show next steps on the path
- Warn of dangers and missteps
- Urge you to pick up the pace, so as not to lose valuable time

The best way to be open to offers of assistance is to keep your quest an open process. When others can see what your pathfinder team is attempting, they will be able to offer assistance at the proper time. Share your adventure with the organization, and create a sense of adventure that others can draw on. Spark interest in others. I have helped pathfinder teams create news notes, build storyboards, hold open houses, report out to interested groups, and sponsor large-group events. Every method you use to share the adventure increases your likelihood of receiving essential offers of help.

Guard Against Holdfasts

Be open to unexpected offers of assistance, yet be careful and trust your best instincts in uncharted territory. Your instincts will tell you when holdfasts are masquerading as helpers. Holdfasts may offer to help, but there will be strings attached. Their offer of help is contingent on your pathfinding team promising to work within the confines of the everyday world.

> In a hospital where a pathfinding team was working on a new care-management approach, a nurse executive offered support. However, she suggested to the pathfinders that the new roles would report through the traditional nursing hierarchy. The result would have been to undermine the new approach in the eyes of the physicians, since they had a contentious history with care managers in the existing hierarchy. The pathfinder team respectfully resisted the offer of assistance. As a result, the physicians overwhelmingly supported the new approach. The result was a true breakthrough, rather than a tweak to the old system.

True helpers on your quest never try to pull you back to the everyday world. Instead, they urge you deeper into new territory.

Someone will help you at a critical point in your quest. You can count on it.

> *The best advisers, helpers and friends always are not those who tell us how to act in special cases, but who give us, out of themselves, the ardent spirit and desire to act right, and leave us then, even through many blunders, to find out what our own form of right action is.*
>
> — *Phillips Brooks, clergyman and author*

Questions for the Quest

1. How will you stay open to helpers on your journey?
2. What specific help does your team need right now?
3. How can your team attract aid inside and outside your organization?
4. What distinguishes a helper from a holdfast? A helper from a mentor?
5. How will you respond to those who offer to help your quest?

11. Path of Trials

The test of an adventure is that when you're in the middle of it, you say to yourself, "Oh, now I've got myself into an awful mess; I wish I were sitting quietly at home."

— Thornton Wilder, playwright and novelist

Life is not easy for any of us. But what of that? We must have perseverance and above all confidence in ourselves. We must believe that we are gifted for something and that this thing must be attained.

— Marie Curie, winner of Nobel prize for physics and chemistry

The path of trials comprises most of the story of the Lewis and Clark Expedition. At every point they encounter obstacles, overcome them, and as a result build critical new capabilities. They will need each of those new capabilities to carry the Corps safely to the breakthrough they are seeking: a route across the continent to the Pacific. The Expedition's trials do not begin when they leave Fort Mandan, but they intensify at that point as the Corps settles into the path of exploration and discovery.

Out in the wilderness, fatal conflicts are now a constant possibility. Several times, they are chased by grizzlies and discover to their horror that the bears are

nearly impossible to bring down with hunting rifles. The boats are at constant risk of capsizing.

Physical obstacles threaten to completely exhaust the men. In one example, the Corps must portage the gear and canoes around five massive cascades on the Missouri River. Broiling heat, hailstorms, swarms of mosquitoes, prickly pear cactus underfoot, and other obstacles mark the difficult portage.

Disappointment can sap the spirit as much as exertion. After crossing the Continental Divide and Lemhi Pass, Lewis and Clark realize that there is no complete water route to the Pacific, no all-water passage that could become a trade route. They must tell the Corps the news and recalibrate the call to adventure that has propelled them this far across the West. As the Corps overcomes these mammoth obstacles, it draws on resources the group has built up earlier in the journey.

Make Your Way to the Prize

Your team has already spent time orienting itself in new territory, consulting new helpers and recommitting to pursuing the path of discovery. Now you are faced with a pivotal stage of the journey where the party must survive, build new capability, and progress toward the goal your team is seeking. At every turn, you and your companions will meet new obstacles and be subjected to new trials or tests of your capability. As your team penetrates deeper into uncharted territory, the obstacles and trials will increase in difficulty.

If a team fails to grow and develop in the tests of the wilderness, the difficulties will overwhelm everyone, and the quest will stall. View this as a challenge rather than a threat. The path of trials is always a test of personal mettle, a time when once-effective leaders stumble and budding leaders step forward.

For these reasons, the path of trials is typically the most exciting and adventuresome stage of the quest. Adventure movies spend most of their time in this phase. Dorothy and her companions must find the Wizard of Oz and pass the trial he gives them, bringing back the witch's broom. Luke Skywalker must find the plans to destroy the Death Star and develop his capabilities under the tutelage of Yoda. Lewis and Clark must cross half an uncharted continent. Your job as pathfinders will be to penetrate the undiscovered areas of your topic and build the capability to eventually make the breakthrough you are seeking for your organization.

Avoid the Project Management Trap

Even though this phase is the hallmark of the quest, it is not included in traditional project management. Traditional projects move directly from planning to execution, as if all the important tasks are already known and agreed upon. Ignoring the path of trials may work for business-as-usual efforts, but on the quest it will ensure that the pathfinders never achieve a breakthrough. Project management is a wonderful tool for known-path projects, like constructing a building, but it is inappropriate for your quest.

In your organizational quest, there will be those who want to create a work breakdown of project steps. This is based on the fatal assumption that the specific steps on a quest can be known in advance. Leaders often make this fatal mistake, which dangerously limits the degrees of freedom so necessary for exploration, discovery and breakthrough. Resist the urge to identify and check off a list of activities for your quest. While project management creates an illusion of control and continuous progress, it is actually a holdfast behavior and will kill your quest.

Assuming that you resist the temptation to misapply project management, others may still expect you to follow project-management protocols. Don't allow your quest to be drawn into the project management trap. Portray it as a path of exploration and discovery.

> I recall an initiative where pathfinder teams were making excellent progress in exploration, when suddenly the executive management group panicked and started asking about steps: *Where is the project plan? Where are the progress reports? Are we getting results yet?* They demanded that the quest leaders produce project management reports, because those reports brought the management team comfort and an illusion of control. At first the pathfinders created the reports that management requested. They soon realized, though, that producing the reports was consuming precious energy that was needed for exploration and discovery. They eventually convinced management to drop the request. The time the teams spent on discovery paid off. They achieved a significant breakthrough that returned the organization to comfortable profitability. No traditionally managed project had ever produced the same magnitude of payback.

One of the saddest moments on a corporate quest is when leaders attempt to hold the pathfinders' feet to the fire by demanding proof of progress. Project management is often a symptom of a checklist culture. This is the opposite of the quest culture. In checklist cultures, leaders are satisfied as long as tasks in the project are checked off on schedule. In the quest culture, be satisfied only if you are making meaningful progress toward your goal.

Every veteran of a quest knows that completing tasks is relatively meaningless. What does matter is discovering concepts or practices that will move you closer to a breakthrough. The specific tasks needed to make those discoveries will remain largely a mystery until earlier actions on the journey are completed. Before your pathfinding team knows what it must do to reach the goal, you will need to absorb the process of learning, discovery and growth. Your team simply cannot be successful on a quest by completing predetermined tasks on time. It must make discoveries that move it closer to the prize. Quests are managed with a compass, not a project stopwatch.

> On one quest at a hospital, where reducing patient length of stay was an overarching objective, management demanded to see consistent progress each month. It was a variation of the checklist problem. If the project lasted ten months, for instance, management wanted to see ten percent of the goal accomplished each month. Management put considerable pressure on the leader of the pathfinder team to report regular progress.
>
> · While that may sound reasonable to a financial manager, it is absurd to an adventurer. Early months on the path of discovery may well lead to useful discoveries that build and multiply until the breakthrough is achieved, but it is impossible to know what percentage of the goal has been reached at that time. It is the breakthrough that creates the big change. Until then, measurable results may be minimal. The pressure to perform according to home-base rules only made the pathfinder team at the hospital feel un-trusted and unsupported. They eventually made a breakthrough in spite of management pressure, achieving length-of-stay reductions that far surpassed management expectations. Even so, hard feelings lingered about the arbitrary pressure to show consistent progress.

Do not let yourself be trapped by checklist mentality. Spend the time to spell out to those concerned how quests are different, and resist conventional project management programs. During the quest, make sure that management knows that you and your pathfinders are not lost or confused. You are not project-managing a proven path. You are leading an adventure of exploration and discovery.

Obstacles Increase in Difficulty

We can see from the Lewis and Clark experience that a number of obstacles impede a team's progress toward the prize. Yet obstacles have extraordinary potential. They test our resolve, provide new opportunities to learn, force us to see with new eyes, and push us to build new capability. Obstacles mark the battle for mastery as the journey unfolds. Early obstacles prepare us for more challenging obstacles yet to come. As we take on the obstacles, we move from solving pieces of the puzzle to creating the whole, where things come together. As we overcome obstacles, we move toward integration and eventually the big breakthrough.

Obstacles test our mettle. If we are too attached to business-as-usual approaches, the obstacles will soon turn into insurmountable barriers. Even if we are open to the journey, the obstacles may challenge us in ways that instigate a personal crisis. Yet even this can be helpful, leading to growth in character and wisdom. Obstacles force us to either abandon the quest or change our way of thinking. When we change our thinking, obstacles become stepping stones.

In legend, overcoming an obstacle meant passing a mysterious test in order to learn the nature of the next level of the adventure, the path to breakthrough. Lancelot had to cross the bridge of swords before he could enter the enchanted castle where Guinevere was being held captive. After surviving the bridge, he realized that he was in love with Guinevere and she with him. Overcoming obstacles makes the seeker worthy of the revelation.

The pathfinding team attempting a breakthrough in reducing patient length of stay had an idea. They wanted to put clinical decision makers – physicians – on the nursing units so that orders could be written and care plans reviewed when admitting physicians (the ones that "owned" the patient) were unavailable. However, the physicians needed for the field trial could not be credentialed within the timeframe needed. Many teams would have stopped there, but this team asked who else could write orders and guide the care plan. They determined that — in their U.S. state, at least — nurse practitioners (NPs) could provide those services under the supervision of the admitting physician.

Another obstacle arose: NPs were in short supply, and they also needed credentialing. But the pathfinding team discovered that the emergency department's physician group was already providing credentialed NPs to the hospital. The physician group agreed to provide NPs for the trial. The trial was a stunning success. It turned out that using the NPs in the new role had many significant advantages over using physicians. Refusing to fall victim to the obstacles, the pathfinder team created a breakthrough.

Faced with a path of trials and refusing to see yourselves as victims, your team can overcome huge obstacles. You will be developing new capabilities that allow you to dramatically improve the system. When one idea is further refined through additional trials and combined with other new concepts, the result can be a breakthrough.

You can think of the path of trials as a spiral discovery process:

1. Conduct preliminary exploration and discovery.
2. Create a preliminary design.
3. Construct and test a trial (or simulation) of the preliminary design.
4. Consolidate discoveries, and strengthen understanding.
5. Evolve the trial (or construct more sophisticated follow-on trials).
6. Determine how to proceed.
7. Evaluate the existing trial in the same way as the previous trials. If necessary, develop another trial from it.
8. Integrate the findings from concurrent trials into higher-level trials.
9. Iterate these steps until you are ready for the ultimate test (see next chapter).

Adventure isn't hanging on a rope off the side of a mountain. Adventure is an attitude that we must apply to the day-to-day obstacles of life: facing new challenges, seizing new opportunities, testing our resources against the unknown and, in the process, discovering our own unique potential.

— John Amatt, organizer and participant in Canada's first successful expedition to summit Mount Everest

Questions for the Quest

1. Make an inventory of occasions when experts brought in a proven-path program from the outside. How many of these programs were successful once the experts left the scene?
2. What strategies would you use to keep the team unfrozen and engaged in discovery?

3. How will you help when the faith, patience, and stamina of the pathfinders are tested?
4. How can your quest be structured so that traditional project management is not an expectation?

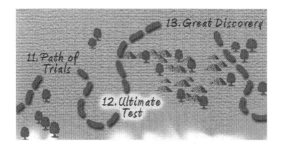

12. Ultimate Test

When you have a crisis, the crisis itself becomes one of your biggest assets if that crisis is bad enough. Everyone gets very modest and humble and listens. If you need to do rough things, you do rough things.

— Carl-Henric Svanberg, CEO, Ericsson

On September 1, 1805, the Corps of Discovery sets out for the Bitterroot Mountains with twenty-nine horses and several mules. The Shoshone people have provided a guide that the captains call Toby. Based on information they gathered, Lewis and Clark believe that a short crossing of the mountain range will take them to rivers that lead to the Pacific. In this way, furs and other goods could later be rather easily portaged between rivers in the east and the westward flowing rivers. They head north toward a mountain pass that will take them into the Bitterroot Valley and then up the Bitterroot Mountains. The prize seems within reach.

But their plans quickly begin unraveling. The trail is nearly impassible with the autumn rains, and the horses fall often. The weather is getting worse daily. The men are cold and wet and often hungry. There is virtually no game for food. They eat a mule and several of their horses.

127

During their trek through the valley, the formidable snow-covered mountains loom large to their left. The men have never seen mountains this terrible. Lewis notes in his journal that they will attempt the crossing on the bare word of Toby, though his fellow Shoshones warn Lewis that passage is impracticable. The Corps must be contemplating that the mountainous crossing in snow and ice will be their doom.

While camping in the Bitterroot Valley, Lewis receives more unsettling information. Toby tells Lewis that by following the Missouri to its source, the Corps missed a shortcut from the Great Falls which could have brought them here in 4 days. Instead, it has taken them 53 days. The Corps lost seven weeks and a chance to cross the Bitterroots in summer weather. Lewis keeps this potentially devastating information to himself.

By September 14, it is clear Toby is lost. He has mistakenly led them down a gully to a fishing camp. The next day, Toby leads the party up a steep ridge. Horses slip on the trail and crash down the ridge, one horse smashing Clark's field desk. Miraculously, the horses escape unhurt. The men expend themselves reaching the ridge. Without water, they need to melt snow.

But the reason that September 15 marks the nadir of the Expedition goes beyond even these terrible proportions. The ultimate challenge is described in the journals. Clark writes, "From this mountain I could observe high rugged mountains in every direction as far as I could see".

Sergeant John Ordway agrees as he writes, "The mountains continue as far as our eyes could extend. They extend much further than we expected." There is no way that the party can cross the mountains before their food runs out. Even if they avoid starvation, a mountain blizzard can easily wipe them out. Any hope for an easy portage to a westward-flowing water route is completely dashed.

Yet to retreat is unthinkable. At this point they prefer to face probable death rather than give up their quest. As a practical matter, they do not even have the supplies or strength to reverse course and return to the Shoshone village. The men are already physically exhausted, cold to the bone, out of food and without hope of finding game. They have reached the moment of probable failure. If they stay in *the mountains they will die. If they turn back they will die. There is no way out but through.*

On September 21, the exhausted and starving men, having split into two groups, stagger out of the mountains and into a welcoming Nez Perce village, a community that nursed them back to health and offered more resources for their journey.

By taking on the Bitterroots in winter, the Corps of Discovery accomplishes one of the incredible feats in American history. The Pacific Ocean is again within reach. When the Corps of Discovery reaches the Nez Perce village, an era ends. Like it or not, they part with their most closely held directive. They need to give up the prospect of finding an almost complete river route to the Pacific. Yet the hopelessness of the Bitterroots passes. They freed themselves from a futile situation. While abandoning the outworn idea of a river route, Lewis and Clark are engaging another dream — they know that they could be the first party to cross the American continent. Their adventure will consolidate American claims on a transcontinental country. In their minds, the era of a transcontinental country has begun.

This Is Your Team's Ultimate Test

As historian Stephen Ambrose points out, "Lewis and Clark had welded the Corps of Discovery into a tough, superbly disciplined family. They had built unquestioning trust in themselves and knew the strengths and skills of each of their men intimately. They had taken a calculated risk in trusting Toby, but their judgment that he knew what he was talking about ... proved to be justified." By leading the Corps through the great crisis of the journey, the captains elevated the crew to the next level.

For every party on a quest, the ultimate test marks the low point, the time of greatest adversity. The quest has reached the crucial state of affairs where there is a distinct possibility of total failure. This low point occurs in organizational quests as well as quests of geographical discovery.

> Most quests have their ultimate test, great crisis or nadir. I worked with a team in an information technology (IT) company. The team set out to devise a new IT development process, only to find out that leadership would not entertain more agile and responsive alternatives to the cumbersome "waterfall" method of development they currently used. This was because the expensive IT project management system only supported waterfall development.
>
> In another example, hospital leaders decided to shut down an employee-driven initiative to create more surgery throughput, because the hospital system had run out of beds and could not handle more surgical patients.

Of course, historians and storytellers have the advantage of identifying the ultimate challenge or great crisis of the story in retrospect. Seen with 20/20 hindsight, the crisis will jump into high relief against the other tests and trials of the quest. But for us to make the idea of an ultimate challenge useful, we have to identify it while it is happening.

Here are some indicators that you and your team have reached that point on your journey:

- You have already invested heavily in the quest. So much will be lost if the quest fails, the idea of stopping is intolerable to the pathfinders. That is why the ultimate test comes toward the end of the discovery phase. By this time, the pathfinders are willing "to die" for the completion of the quest. On other quests, this death can be quite literal. It was a probable consequence for the Corps of Discovery.

In organizational quests, death is not physical but could well mean killing career opportunities or losing your job.

- An apparently insurmountable obstacle stands between you and the breakthrough. There is no way to avoid the dilemma and still accomplish the mission of the quest. If there is another way, then consider backing up and taking a route around the obstacle. The Corps tried for nearly two months to find the best route around the great rapids on the way up to the Bitterroots.

- Your retreat has been cut off. If you cannot back up and take another route, then the only way out is through the crisis. Once they were in the middle of the Bitterroots, Lewis and Clark had neither the strength nor the supplies to retrace their route. For a pathfinder team in the cruise line industry, it appeared that they could not create regional teams to handle the incoming reservation calls, simply because of an outdated phone computer. The pathfinder team found they had no choice but to make regional teams work with the old phone computer.

- It is a dark night of the soul. The ultimate test is emotionally unsettling at best and unhinging at worst. By the point of an ultimate test, the pathfinders have had to endure significant hardship and have made deep emotional commitments to the success of their quest. The thought of losing it all is very disturbing. Spirits collapse. This is often the time leaders crack and fail to provide steady guidance. Imagine the frame of mind of Lewis and Clark after they hear that they wasted seven weeks of favorable weather getting to the Bitterroots. Their steadiness in the face of the crisis is a triumph of leadership.

- There is a surprising setback. Things were going well and then, without warning, fortunes are reversed. Earlier progress is undone. I worked with a team in healthcare that was radically redesigning how the hospital nursing units communicated with physicians. The trials had produced marvelous results. Then the team discovered that a key part of the technology could not comply with legislation on patient confidentiality, in spite of earlier reassurances from the vendor.

- The journey is simply getting stale. Nothing is working. Trials and experiments are no longer yielding useful results. There is no one event that the pathfinders can point to, but nothing seems to move the party forward toward their goal. Time is ticking, and yet the journey is going nowhere. The pathfinders are stuck in the doldrums.

If you find yourself in the ultimate test, be ready to take these actions:

- The crisis may demand a radical re-orientation of your ideas. You may need to change the goals of the quest. For example, Ernest Shackleton changed his goal from crossing Antarctica to getting all his crew to safety, after pack ice crushed the ship and they had to find a way home with no vessel. You may have to let go of beliefs, behaviors and techniques that you brought with you from the business-as-usual world. For example, a pathfinder team seeking to change the operations of a mother-baby unit had to let go of the idea that induced deliveries were undesirable and should be restricted before they could again proceed. Remember that many people who get lost in the woods fail to understand where they are because they don't reorient their mental maps to their true location. This is the last chance to challenge your closely held assumptions and re-orient your map.

- Temporarily suspend your stated plans. Attempts to control the path must fail by this point. Current plans may embody outmoded assumptions and out-of-date information. It is all too easy to deny the ultimate test and doggedly carry on with your plans. Suspending your plans reduces the possibility of thoughtless actions and creates the open space for revised or improvised plans. Use your resilience to adapt to the quickly changing situation. Devise an interim short-term crisis plan.

- You may be on the wrong path but still have time to change. Consider where your group may have made a wrong turn on their path of discovery. Fortunately for Lewis and Clark, Toby recognized his error and could guide them on a new course. Review your path carefully, looking for possible wrong turns. This is not to say that you should change paths willy-nilly, but consider a different path if you have evidence that your team is lost.

- Avoid the temptation to over-control. At this crisis point, you may feel significant loss of control. It is natural to compensate by redoubling your efforts to impose control. Remember that during a crisis things are shifting quickly; the situation is in flux. Loosen control so new information is quickly available and so those with unique information or expertise have the freedom to get involved immediately. Let new possibilities emerge.

- Be ready to deal with old wounds. Often, team members will set aside differences and conflict during your quest. But this can re-emerge with startling ferocity during the ultimate test. Team members may blame each other for the current situation. Re-focus the group on the situation and the overarching goal. Remind people of the trust that has been built between the team members. Be ready to take decisive action.

- Be open to helpers. Lewis and Clark depended on Toby to guide them through the Bitterroots. When they came out of the mountains, the Nez Perce took care of them. Time and again, someone emerged to help the pathfinder teams I have consulted when times were tough. Seek out help, and do not let an authentic offer of help go unconsidered.

- When free of the crisis, move toward your goal. Your team has pulled together to overcome the ultimate test; they have tapped their deepest inner resources and overcome acute fears. They have had a profound experience that has taken them to the next level. Instead of conducting more trials, move on to the goal; attempt the big change.

Those who survive the ultimate test retain accountability and take a heroic stance in the face of crisis. Others become victims. Taking a heroic stance means asking these questions:

- What is this situation about? Do I have all the information I need? What is my gut telling me? Are my assumptions appropriate; is my mental model of the overall plan correct?

- How can I remedy this situation? What are my options?

- How can I still achieve my goal even in my current situation? How can I rise above these circumstances and achieve the object of the quest in spite of these extreme obstacles?

Passing the ultimate test has enormously positive results. As philosopher Friedrich Nietzsche famously said, "What doesn't kill us makes us stronger." The ultimate test provides an agonizing opportunity for deep growth, to integrate the insights from recent trials, and to examine old habits and outmoded thinking. Pathfinders gain self-confidence by taking unified and decisive action in the face of overwhelming adversity.

Imagine if Lewis and Clark had not needed to face the Bitterroots. The crisis survived provides great power. It is easy to imagine how their newfound power may have protected them on the rest of the journey. Having survived your ultimate test, you are now ready to take on future challenges.

Questions for the Quest

1. How will you recognize the ultimate test on your quest?
2. Name a leader you admire. How did this person lead through times of great crisis?
3. Are you ready to figuratively die (put your career at risk) to see the quest succeed?
4. What outmoded ideas, perceptions and information are you still carrying forward at this stage of your quest? How can you dispose of these to lighten the load?
5. In what ways can the ultimate test strengthen your pathfinding team?

Threshold of Discovery

Breakthrough

Section Three: Breakthrough

Breakthrough! By this point your quest has culminated in the great discovery that holds the potential to renew the organization. It was an immense effort to get this far – it is hard to imagine being capable of this breakthrough before the quest began. Now, just when your team is most capable, it must make the decision to turn for home with the prize. The return path will be no cakewalk, but the potential rewards are immense, making the effort worthwhile.

The Breakthrough Phase, comprising the third quadrant of the quest landscape, takes place in uncharted territory. It begins with your achievement of the big breakthrough. This breakthrough represents a turning point, wrapping up expansionary exploration and refocusing the group on mastering the breakthrough, before returning with the prize to home base.

The Breakthrough phase can be a dangerous return because there is a tendency for pathfinders to relax; knowing they have achieved a breakthrough and assuming the homeward journey will be trouble-free. Just as most mountain climbing accidents happen on the descent, pathfinders are easily caught off guard by the perils of the return. During Breakthrough pathfinders balance the tension between taking the time for mastery and moving quickly to adoption.

The Great Discovery

The great discovery marks the breakthrough that allows the pathfinders to accomplish the big change. The great discovery may be a one-time breakthrough or the successful integration of many earlier innovations. In either case, it represents a major advance in the pathfinders' knowledge and capability. They now have what they need, in raw form, to renew the organization. The great discovery is the culmination of pathfinders' exploration. Now they must work to put the breakthrough to use.

Turning Point

During the Exploration Phase, the journey opened out toward increasing possibilities. After the great discovery it is time to turn for home. As the pathfinders make the turn, expansion must give way to consolidation. Consolidation concludes with returning home with the great discovery. This milestone represents a recommitment to the great discovery and forecloses continuing exploration.

Mastery in Two Worlds

During mastery, the pathfinders develop sufficient command of their discovery to extend its capability so they can soon apply its power for routine use in the everyday world. At the Great Discovery milestone, they discovered that the "big change" was possible. Now they must reproduce the big change under real-life conditions. The pathfinders learn precisely how their discovery works transitioning from an experimental model to a robust design. During this period pathfinders deepen their understanding and control, integrate more pieces, try variations and extensions, and prepare to share their breakthrough with the organization.

Race Against Time

Pathfinders are sometimes tempted to delay their return in order to carry out more exploration. However, by now time is working against them, and they linger at their peril. The state of misfortune may be deepening or the window of opportunity closing. Delays can diminish the team's relevancy or allow it to be overtaken by competitive approaches. Home base will not wait. The pathfinders must win the race against time to make a triumphant return possible.

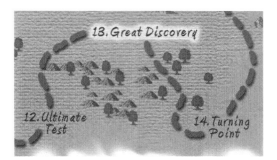

13. Great Discovery

13. Great Discovery

It's hard for corporations to understand that creativity is not just about succeeding. It's about experimenting and discovering.
— Gordon Mackenzie, author of *Orbiting the Giant Hairball*

Weakened from their crossing of the Bitterroots and suffering from serious intestinal illness (probable food poisoning), the aptly named Corps of Discovery, using newly built dugout canoes, navigates the many treacherous rapids of the upper Columbia River. Canoeing these rapids, which at the time contain steep waterfalls, is a feat the natives warned them was impossible. Miraculously, they succeed and eventually enter the smoother waters of the lower Columbia. On November 7, 1805, the Corps of Discovery floats down the Columbia River to the point where it widens into an estuary. Clark, believing he sees the Pacific, writes, "Ocian (sic) in View! O the joy."

In reality, the Corps is still miles from the Pacific, but that is a minor concern. The crew knows that the ocean is immediately ahead. Later, pinned down on the north bank in an area they dub Dismal Nitch, they are treated to fierce storms generating howling winds, high waves, and no harbor. Though they are now only about three miles from the ocean, it takes the party several weeks to actually stand on the shores of the Pacific. The quest is only half over, since the Corps must still survive a treacherous return home. But Lewis and Clark have achieved the prize they sought: cross-continental passage to the Pacific.

The Prize Can Take Many Forms

Every quest has its Holy Grail, the great prize that is the object of a difficult or extended journey of discovery. For Lewis and Clark, the great prize was attaining a trail to the Pacific Ocean, which guaranteed the possibility of an American trade route with the Far East.

For pathfinders on an organizational quest, the prize can take many forms. Think of inventors and adventurers who have discovered the marvelous element through various paths:

- A breakthrough idea (Isaac Newton's theory of gravity)
- Sudden and tremendous synergy (Apollo 13 crew averting crises through teamwork)
- A big change that finally works after much experimentation (Edison's light bulb)
- A conceptual or performance breakthrough (Nadia Comenic's first-time-ever perfect 10 scores in 1972 Olympics gymnastics)
- A successful new design element (Frank Lloyd Wright's modern buildings)
- A seed for a cultural reorientation (the Beatles' breakthrough onto the world music scene)
- The means to thrust into a new business area (Starbucks brings espresso to the masses)
- A new alliance (Kinko's meets FedEx)

The Prize Holds the Promise of Renewed Vitality

Whatever form it takes, the prize is the source of renewed vitality for the community. In Lewis and Clark's case, their prize freed a country from its geographic confines and fueled the epic westward expansion of the United States. The pathfinders' prize of the quest fuels the revitalization of its organization back home.

I have personally worked with organizations that attained prizes allowing them to create new cultures, design breakthrough processes, create new lines of business, clear logjams in their organizations, and offer new services. The prize is always the means to new vitality, never an end in itself. The end, of course, requires the completion and fulfillment of the quest. As with the Corps of Discovery, pathfinders are only halfway there once they achieve the prize.

An amazing fact is that the prize conveys little power of its own. The power comes from the journey to achieve it. It comes from the new capability that was honed through experience, trials and obstacles that pathfinders overcome on the quest itself. In fact, the prize can even be harmful if the pathfinders are not capable of using it.

Imagine two sled dog teams arriving neck and neck at the finish line of the great Iditarod sled race. Now imagine hearing that one of those teams had just arrived fresh from a cargo plane ride from Anchorage and only spent the last mile on the ground. Which team deserves the prize, and which team deserves to be discredited?

When pathfinders show themselves to be creditable adventurers, they can use their newfound prize to great effect. Your team attains the ultimate prize when you have built your capabilities sufficiently. When you can put your lessons together in a unique way, you will see the implications for the organization. It is now time to stop searching and starting consolidating your discoveries. It is the synthesis of the insights and capabilities gained to this point that will create a powerful new source of vitality. The prize is the quest's invention.

For an international airport pathfinding team, the quest prize was new information. The pathfinders set their ultimate goal as creating extraordinary levels of customer service as measured by a recognized international survey. They wanted to be in a very exclusive club, among the top ten airports in the world. The two available airport surveys associated high levels of customer service with facilities, services, and efficiency. However, the pathfinders' own research, using innovative techniques for customer research, pointed out an undiscovered dimension: the capability and willingness of the airport to help solve individual traveler problems. The pathfinders realized that they had the prize; they took advantage of a dimension of satisfaction that other airports had overlooked and soared to the top five spot.

Test for the Great Discovery

The great discovery is the highest achievement set before the pathfinders. Ironically, however, it is not always easy to know that your team has arrived and discovered the marvelous prize. "X" doesn't necessarily mark the spot. Perhaps the team has only found an intermediate discovery, not the ultimate prize. Imagine an archaeological team that sets out to find a new dinosaur skeleton, only to stop work when it uncovers the first bone!

Here are some tests to find out whether your team has actually found the prize:

- Things are working together. The prize integrates various elements your team has been working on. Pieces that seemed impossibly disconnected now fit together in surprising and satisfying ways.

- There is a new level of power and harmony that was previously far beyond the reach of the team. The potential that was hoped for is now available.
- The team senses a new clarity and centeredness. Here, the pathfinders can see the means to the end. There is finally a sense that the path is true and that the search for a breakthrough is over.

What Now?

Attaining the prize brings a sense of new possibilities. The pathfinders have achieved the means to align what was in disarray, balance what was unstable, repair what was broken, and create what was once unimaginable.

Once the Corps of Discovery reached the Pacific Ocean, they could go no further. After wintering at Fort Clatsop, they would head for home. In the same way, pathfinder teams in organizations must now ask themselves if it is time to turn for home. This means winding up the expansionary activities of the discovery phase and moving into a phase of consolidation and integration.

So, while attaining the prize is a time of great joy and relief, it may also be a time of melancholy. It is hard to let go of the excitement of discovery and buckle down to work on the new endeavors of integration and mastery.

Waiting through the rainy, cold winter at Fort Clatsop on the Pacific Coast was the most depressing time for the Corps. Likewise, the time after achieving the prize may be depressing for your fellow pathfinders. It's hard to let go of discovery. Some never do. We call them consultants.

Time is Short

The window of opportunity is closing. After celebrating their success and verifying that the prize is true, the demands of the quest to return home will draw the pathfinders forward again. A ceremony will help mark this point of return. Pathfinders know that, fortified with the prize, they hold the power to achieve renewal. It's time to make the turn for home – the return is fraught with its own hazards – there is no time to waste.

Many organizations, armed with consultant-provided proven-path methodologies, attempt to steal the prize – that is, to gain the prize without partaking in a quest at all. Without the perceived cost, time and disruption of a quest, leaders may choose to buy the source of vitality.

In some cases, the consultants can deliver the prize to the organization without the need for the organization to explore, build new capability, and eventually discover the prize. However, without the quest and the resulting development of new capability, the organization will not be capable of sustaining the benefits of the prize; the consultants leave, and soon the benefits fade into the organizational lore of yet another initiative gone awry. In myth and legend, false heroes who attempt to steal the prize are ultimately destroyed because they are not worthy. They have tried to shortcut the process without gaining tools and experience along the way. Gaining the prize by traveling on the quest is the only way to create lasting vitality.

Questions for the Quest

1. What is the prize for your particular quest? Does the prize need to be redefined?
2. How will you know that you have attained the breakthrough and not made just an intermediate discovery?
3. Why is the breakthrough not available to everyone? How have you become capable of achieving it?

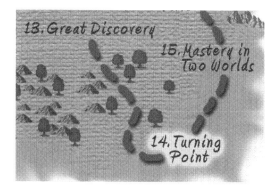

14. Turning Point

So after the quest of the Sangreal was fulfilled, and all knights
that were left alive were come again unto the Table Round ...
then was there great joy in the court.

— Thomas Malory, 15th c. English
author or compiler of *Le Morte d'Arthur*

*Turning for home is perilous in every quest; that was certainly true for the
Lewis and Clark Expedition. As they set out for home on March 23, 1806, their
resources were nearly depleted. They were only halfway through their journey, but
they had consumed ninety-five percent of their supplies. So desperate was their situation that Lewis broke his own moral code and authorized the theft of a canoe from
a tribe. Lewis soon learned from the natives that there was a great food shortage on
the river and people upstream were starving. If the Expedition waited for several
weeks for the beginning of the salmon run, they would miss their rendezvous with
the Nez Perce to retrieve their horses and would also jeopardize their ability to get
onto the Missouri River before it froze the following autumn.*

Making their way up the Columbia, they were constantly harassed by the starving natives, who often stole from the party or attempted to do so. Lewis lost his temper on several occasions, twice threatened to kill, and threatened to torch native houses. If he had followed through on his threats, he would have severely damaged relations with a valuable ally and jeopardized the safety of the Corps of Discovery. Both the Corps and the natives were at the breaking point, but fortunately major conflict was avoided.

They made their rendezvous with the Nez Perce but the horses were not available as promised. A dispute between two chiefs resulted in the scattering of the horses. After much negotiation, many of the horses and saddles were eventually recovered.

On May 7, 1806, the party caught sight of the Bitterroots for the first time since leaving them in September 1805. The Nez Perce told Lewis that the winter had brought unusually heavy snow and the mountains would not be passable until June or even later. Their return was blocked. The Corps would have to wait for at least three weeks. Getting back home with the prize is never easy.

The Pieces Are Fitting Together

Returning with your great discovery to home base will be perilous, but obviously for different reasons than those of the Corps. The good news is that things are working and the pieces are fitting together. You are mastering the discovery and deepening your understanding. It is time to return home so you can share the gift. But the unwelcome news is that you may be running out of time, resources, and support. Moreover, there may be organizational forces blocking your return. You must continue to act decisively so as not to get stuck.

Beware of Perils of the Return

The return holds many obstacles and hazards for the organizational pathfinder team. Turning for home represents a change of state from divergent exploration to the convergent process of bringing the prize home. As with all systems, the change of state is the period of greatest risk of failure. Just when the quest team wants to relax and enjoy its newfound discovery, the risk increases. At the time when leaders are tempted to assume their job is done, the need for leadership is heightened. Just as the fairy tales tell us, finding our way out of the forest is risky business. This is a time that requires mindfulness and attention to detail; a surprising collapse is all too easy.

As I have noted previously, some pathfinders are so obsessed with their new discovery that they refuse to close off the quest. They prefer to linger, allowing themselves to delve deeper and deeper into the meaning and power of the new discovery. Lingering with the prize can be extremely rewarding. It can strengthen a personal sense of growth, mastery, and power. There is a natural inner resistance to moving on. Why not wait a bit longer to exploit the full power of the discovery? Fortunately for Lewis and Clark, wintering over at a hastily built Fort Clatsop near the northwest tip of present-day Oregon was such a miserably cold and rainy experience that no one was willing to delay. Lewis had carefully planned for the first feasible day when the Corps could start the return. Plan for the point of return; encourage your team to press ahead. Do not strive for perfection. Return quickly with a workable solution.

Some teams simply lose their way. They become overwhelmed with the detail work needed to prepare for adoption of the prize in the everyday world. What was doable in theory seems Lilliputian in relation to the need to make a full-scale implementation of the practice back at home base.

If this happens to your team, reach out for helpers. Helpers can appear to support the quest at any point. Break the work into doable pieces, then work concurrently to conquer the details. Even

Lewis and Clark divided the Corps into two groups on their return, so as to cover more territory without wasting time.

There is always the possibility of succumbing to an inner adversary. Discovery is often a peak moment for the pathfinders. The creative people who thrived in the discovery phase might disengage on the return leg. They may see the return as a time when discovery is replaced by containment, refinement, and detailed planning for eventual adoption. Many discovery-oriented people cannot tolerate the pedestrian nature of detail planning. If the detail work is overwhelming, consider adding a few people who thrive on the details of planning.

The people and organizational forces (the holdfasts) that impeded your departure might now act to block your return. The change you bring back can represent a threat to the status quo that they seek to protect. So do not be surprised if people attempt to kill the adoption of your discovery, even before you are ready with a plan.

You must be an advocate, ready to demonstrate and promote your discovery when you arrive home. Success requires both a better idea and a constituency. Build constituency aggressively before it is time to approve adoption. Never assume that the facts will carry the day, since others will not hold the same understanding or depth of conviction as the returning pathfinders who have experienced the quest. You will need to promote and defend your discovery.

Running out of time is such a common threat that I dedicated a separate chapter to the topic. Suffice to say here that when teams feel time slipping through their fingers, they may take reckless action. Those who cut back on the scope and scale of their discovery, in order to save time, are settling for mediocrity. The purpose of any quest is renewed vitality, not just an uninspired improvement.

Protect the integrity of your discovery by moving quickly to provide a smooth path for adoption.

Teams sometimes run into unanticipated consequences of their discovery. At worst, these consequences are harmful, requiring countermeasures or even disabling part of the great discovery. At best they require time and resources to understand the consequences and exploit any benefits. You can minimize these surprises by looking for unintended consequences in the mastery phase. When you test and verify your discovery, make sure that you are trying to identify unexpected effects.

As you refine your use of the discovery, look for surprising outcomes. An emergency-room department pathfinder team was surprised to discover that dramatically reducing delays resulted in seeing a higher proportion of highly acute cases. It wasn't long before they found the reason: emergency vehicle drivers, very concerned for their patients, had begun requesting that particular ER from the emergency dispatcher.

Whatever perils you may face, your return will be full of adventure. This is a time on the journey when you can expand your awareness of the discovery and how its powers will play out when you share it with the rest of the organization. Be observant. For example, even as Lewis and Clark headed home, Lewis carefully observed and recorded the flora and fauna and cultures of the natives. The return is not a heedless rush for home but a time to move deliberately and without pause. You, too, will have much to do on your return journey. Use the return to prepare for the next phase: sharing your prize and moving into its adoption.

Prepare for Home

At this point in your quest, your team will need to focus on what is most necessary, as you bring the prize back to home base.

Keep explorations to a minimum now. Entertain new divergent exploration only under extraordinary circumstances. The primary design work of the return is to prepare for adoption of the great discovery, the prize.

> While a pathfinder team in surgery was consolidating their redesigns to the surgical process, they realized they might be able to change the process for establishing a sterile field in the operating room. The new process would save precious time setting up for the next case. However, pursuing the opportunity meant delaying the adoption of the more crucial design changes. They chose to identify the sterile-field issue for another time.

Consolidate the gains. You may need to integrate all your discoveries into a whole, ready for everyday use. While pathfinders can often see clearly how the prize can be used at home base, there may still be many loose ends in the design. What works under trial conditions, under the watchful eye of your pathfinder team, may not work in everyday service. The team may have to pull the pieces together into a unified package and add elements that make the new discovery easier to use. As your team spends more time using their discovery on the return trip, you will learn how to set it up for everyday use.

Strengthen and simplify the design. Once you have pulled all the pieces together, it is an excellent time to get rid of the extraneous pieces that do not serve the consolidated design. For example, once a home loan processing team discovered how to reduce appraisal turnaround time from about three weeks to less than three days, they realized they did not need complicated ordering and scheduling systems for appraisals. Take out what is not necessary in routine daily use. Then add new structure to strengthen the design so it will work under a wide range of conditions with a wide range of users.

Reconnect with the organization. During the return journey you will want to reestablish contact with people and groups that may have lost touch with your quest and its progress. Communicate your progress thus far and the results of your efforts.

Spark some interest in the organization. Hold an open house where others can view your discovery. Stage a demonstration of the prize. Recreate your key experiment. Begin presenting at organizational forums and meetings. Reveal your results. One group I worked with had immersion sessions, inviting people to a day-long, hands-on demonstration of their discovery. Let the organization know that you have succeeded and that you are nearing completion of your quest. If you shock people with a triumphant return that is unexpected, they will resist your ideas.

Plan for adoption. Beyond strengthening your new design, you will need to plan for adoption of your discovery. Consider doing the following:

- Set the scope of the implementation. Ask yourselves, "Who are the adoption candidates, and how will we spread the adoption over time?"

- Create a time schedule for implementation. Determine how long you think the adoption will take, along with the timing of the major milestones.
- Initiate implementation communications. Make contact with the people who would manage and support the adoption efforts, and begin talks about potential adoption efforts.
- Determine any impact on human resource and organizational policies. Estimate adjustments that the organization will need to make to accommodate your discovery.
- Create design specifications for the system. If your discovery changes systems, specify how the systems will be different.
- Identify resources. Determine what resources (people, supplies, equipment, facilities, etc.) will be required for adoption.

Fend off attacks. Unfortunately, the more imminent your return, the more the naysayers and holdfast forces will resist and attack your discovery. Engaging the organization immediately upon your return will help lessen the attacks. Work hard to build constituency for adoption of your discovery. Do not expect it to be accepted on its technical merits.

In one case, pathfinders on a pharmacy project discovered how to save time, reduce dangerous medical errors, and save hundreds of thousands of dollars by changing the way medications were ordered. They borrowed the high-resolution fax equipment they had proposed and held "open houses" to demonstrate the new technology to pharmacists, nurses, physicians, and administrators.

> The administrators who at first couldn't see the need for a "fancy $5000 fax machine" soon ordered thirty.

Know who supports your discovery and who discourages it. Make every effort to expand your support. Ask for the active support of the initial sponsor of the quest. Address criticisms directly and calmly. Restate your overall goals, your demonstrated results, and the potential to create new vitality for the organization. Let people know how your discovery will heal an existing state of misfortune in the organization. There are no better advocates for the discovery than your own pathfinding team.

Pick up the pace. Once you begin reconnecting with the organization, it will expect forthcoming results. Delays will sap your momentum for adoption. Make every effort to stay on track so as to build confidence within the organization. The organization may (and usually does) choose to delay adoption for its own reasons, but it expects the pathfinders to be ready to adopt as soon as they return.

Turning for home puts you on the path to cross back over the threshold of adventure, back into the everyday world where the old rules are still king. Curb your urge to keep exploring, and begin the path home. There is still plenty to accomplish before you will be ready to share your great discovery with those back at home base. If you have not begun already, now is the time to move into mastery of that discovery.

Questions for the Quest

1. What hazards might you face as you turn for home base?
2. How will you prepare before arriving home?

3. How will you address the forces that oppose the changes you are proposing?
4. How do your actions during the return shape your homecoming?

15. Mastery in Two Worlds

If one is master of one thing and understands one thing well, one has, at the same time, insight into and understanding of many things.
— Vincent Van Gogh, Dutch post-Impressionist artist

Substantive abandonment of convention is evidence of mastery.
— Eric Parslow, author

Lewis and Clark begin the process of mastery even before starting the return leg of their great trek. Clark completes a comprehensive map of their route. After going over the map with Clark, Lewis writes on February 14, "We now discover that we have found the most practicable and navigable passage across the Continent of North America." How they could know for a fact that their passage is the best — when they tried only one route — is open to debate, but their summary of the route is the first of its kind, presenting an excellent argument.

In fact, they continue to deepen their knowledge of the overland routes and their knowledge of the flora, fauna, geography, and native people on their return journey. Lewis and Clark already have a general feel of the territory but now use their return trip to refine their information and add new details. In one case, Lewis describes in great detail the lives of the Clatsop and Chinook people. Tragically, within a year of that account, the tribes are virtually wiped out by smallpox and malaria acquired from contact with ships' crews.

The implications of the great discovery of the route are momentous. True, President Jefferson's hope for a navigable East-West water route across the continent — with only a short portage from the Missouri River to the Columbia River — is not to be found. Historian John Allen noted that Lewis and Clark's realization of this fact was a great "transformation of geographical lore." Yet Jefferson will welcome the truth over speculation.

Within fifty years, the approximate route of the Corps will be developed with the Oregon Trail. Steel rails and telegraph wires will connect the country. Lewis and Clark have no way of predicting the railroad and telegraph, but they do understand that the future course of American expansion is now set. Once they reached the Pacific, it was as if they knew the once-insignificant United States had become a legitimate transcontinental country. Surely, Lewis and Clark realized the potential. Even though they did not find the mythical East-West water route across the continent, they mastered the significance of their bittersweet discovery.

Study the Implications of Your Prize

Lewis and Clark were able to consider the implications of their discovery: a viable overland route to the Pacific. They used the time at the turning point to prepare their report for President Jefferson. After the turning point, they continued to deepen and refine their knowledge and understanding. Likewise, your pathfinding team needs to use the time after turning for home base to explore the capabilities and implications of your great discovery. This is the time for mastery. Mastery involves deepening your understanding and studying the implications of your discovery. You can do this in a number of ways:

- Debrief with your team of pathfinders.
- Fit pieces together by trying variations and extensions.
- Integrate the discovery with other systems.
- Control the discovery in a wide range of conditions.
- Assess the impact and long-range potential of the discovery.

Repeatability is the heart of mastery. In the mastery phase, start with an experimental or provisional use of the prize. Then move through experiments to create an application that is robust, able to work as expected under the wide variety of conditions that could be expected in your organization back home. When you master the prize, you will be confident that you can make it work in the real world. You must be master in two worlds: the experimental world of discovery and the applied world of everyday use.

Mastery is a process of experimentation aimed toward refinement. The methods that served the pathfinders during the discovery phase still apply here. Build experiments that push the limits of your new discovery. Find out what it can do; find its breaking point. If the number of variables becomes overwhelming, consider design-of-experiments tools to control the complexity. If you cannot build field experiments, try walk-through simulations or computer simulations. Before moving on, verify that you can achieve the prize's benefits under real-world conditions.

> I worked with a pathfinding team that developed a medical device for detecting retained sponges in surgical patients. We built several prototypes and successfully demonstrated their effectiveness in a "test bench" setting. Then the refinement experiments began. Does it work best with wrist or body electrodes? How far can the electrodes be placed from the incision? How deep in the body will the device work? Does it interfere with any other equipment? Is it easy to sterilize? The list goes on. Without first getting answers to these questions, pathfinders know that the prize is obviously not ready to use in an operating room. The intellectual distance between attaining the prize and mastering the use of the prize can be significant.

While mastery and the resulting refinement are common in science, mastery is often resisted in the corporate world. Invariably, this is the step in the journey that leadership wants to truncate or skip altogether, in the rush to implement the prize. As a result, inventions often get rushed into production without enough trials, and new software is applied without enough time to search for bugs.

The outbound, expansive period of discovery seems to cause a high degree of anticipation in those in the organization back at home base, waiting for results. By the time of the great discovery, those back home may be focused on quick results, not mastery. For that reason, after your pathfinding team celebrates attaining your prize, be prepared to receive pressure to move quickly into implementation — you may even be asked to skip most or all of mastery. Many reasons are given for the sudden increase in pressure to return to home base:

"We're behind schedule and need to pick up the pace."
"You can always refine the prize during implementation."
"Support is waning. You need to show results now."

Don't Skip the Mastery Phase

No matter how strong the pressure, though, remind the team and those back home that mastery of the great discovery is key to the success of the whole initiative. Without mastery, you have neither repeatability nor the robustness to make the prize create breakthroughs in everyday application. By skipping the mastery phase, pathfinders run the very real risk of failure during later implementation. This will waste the effort of the quest and can have severe business and career consequences.

As a consultant, I worked with several teams in an information technology shop trying out a new approach to IT solution development. The teams spent several months working concurrently on different aspects of the new design. When it came time to master the connections between the elements and verify performance, management grew impatient and directed the teams to move directly into implementation. While the implementation was not a total disaster, it was rocky. There were many false starts and on-the-fly redesigns that could have been avoided. The results fell short of the breakthrough we desired. Much of the potential of employee innovation was not realized. Without taking the time to master the breakthrough, the rush to implementation undermined breakthrough thinking.

While it could be fatal to skip the mastery stage, it is also essential not to prolong the process. The interest of mastery can create an urge to linger. Move as quickly as possible through the activities needed to make sure that the benefits of the prize are repeatable at home base. When you can say "yes" to the following questions, it is time to head for home base:

- Are the pieces properly connected and integrated?
- Are all the pieces working and contributing to the overall benefit?
- Have non-contributing elements of an initial design been scrapped or redesigned?
- Can you realize the full benefits of the discovery under a realistic range of conditions?
- Have you accounted for the negative consequences of the new approach?
- Is the profound insight that forms the essence of the breakthrough still evident?

When you make the great discovery, you also gain the clarity to see to the end of the quest. You will want to consider the consequences of your breakthrough. After Clark made the complete map of their passage during the Expedition, he and Lewis looked ahead all the way to a future conversation with President Jefferson. It was time to revisit their ultimate goal and evaluate whether or not the prize had the power to achieve it. How would Lewis present the report, and how would Jefferson receive it? In some ways, their great discovery was a deep disappointment, because they had found no cross-continent water route. But in countless other ways, their quest had profound and lasting importance. Take this interlude to look to the end of your quest and assess the impact of your prize on those back home.

How will your discovery compare to the ultimate goal of the quest, as set out in the call to adventure? There are several possibilities:

1. The prize will allow you to achieve the ultimate, stated goal of your quest. Terrific! Pull up stakes, and head for home.
2. You will fall short of your stated goal but still achieve significant, even breakthrough, benefits. You will still create new vitality in your organization. Reset your goals, and turn for home.
3. You will fall significantly short of your stated goal, Are there other benefits to be gained by continuing mastery? Did you mistake an interim discovery for the great prize? If so, do you have the resources to renew discovery? If not, how can you and your organization learn and grow as a result of your quest? Having to settle for learning and growth without a major breakthrough is always a possibility on the quest, but outright failure is only assured by never starting out on the quest. If you fall short of your objective, do what all adventurers do: use what you have learned from your experience, and create a new call to a better quest.
4. Your discovery greatly exceeds the stated goal. Congratulations! This outcome is not an uncommon one. If your team has time to spend, consider recalibrating your quest to take full advantage of your discovery. You may even decide to propose a second quest.

Be open to the possibility that you have discovered something much bigger than you intended, even if your results look disappointing at first. This was certainly the case with Lewis and Clark.

As part of a quest, a pathfinder team invented a way to transfer a sterile field into an operating room, rather than set it up inside the operating room while delaying the next case. Whereas their goal was to reduce operating room turnover time, the team realized that the invention had other profound implications. This discovery later led to the construction of two surgical facilities that incorporated the invention.

During this phase in most quests, pathfinders also discover a personal sense of mastery. Since the outset of the quest, they have faced challenges and overcome obstacles, replaced ignorance with insight, and conquered feelings of self-limitation. Where they were inflexible, they now seek novelty and change. Where they were stagnating in their old roles, they feel more engaged than ever. By this point, the pathfinders are powerful people with newfound capability. They expect more of themselves, and they will demand respect when they return home with the great discovery. A noteworthy aspect of the quest is unlocking human potential and allowing employee-driven innovation.

The great thing and the hard thing is to stick to things when you have outlived the first interest, and not yet got the second, which comes with a sort of mastery.
— *Janet Erskine Stuart, education expert*

Questions on the Quest

1. What do you risk if your pathfinding team skips mastery and moves straight to implementation?
2. How can further experiments refine your newly discovered breakthrough?
3. What are the indicators that your team's mastery is increasing?
4. What are other possible short-term and long-term applications of the breakthrough?
5. If your discovery doesn't attain the goals of your quest, what are your options? What will you do if your discovery exceeds the goals of your quest?

17. Sharing the Breakthrough

16. Race Against Time

15. Mastery in Two Worlds

16. Race against Time

We must use time as a tool, not as a crutch.
— John F. Kennedy, 35th U.S. President

The only reason for time is so that everything doesn't happen at once.
— Albert Einstein, 1921 Nobel Prize winner in physics

Time, or the lack thereof, threatened to undo the Lewis and Clark Expedition on many occasions. For example, between 1804 and 1806 the Spanish, in order to protect their claims from intrusions by the United States, launched four expeditions from Santa Fe in failed attempts to find and arrest Lewis and Clark. The last of these expeditions included more than 400 Spanish soldiers and Indian allies. Yet Lewis and Clark had no idea that they were being pursued. At a crucial river crossing on the return trip, the Spanish were only days behind the Corps. Had Lewis and Clark lingered there just a few days, the Spanish could have easily wiped them out. Without even being aware of it, Lewis and Clark were truly engaged in a race against time across still-unknown territory toward home.

Don't Lose Track of Time

One of the toughest lessons I have had to learn when guiding my clients on quests is this: every quest is a race against time across unknown territory. Time continues to race by, regardless of the circumstances of the pathfinders.

Time is the most valuable thing a pathfinding team can spend. Somewhere back at home base, someone continues to suffer because the quest is not yet complete. If the pathfinders begin to dawdle during their adventure, the need for the quest will eventually pass and the quest will be irrelevant. Most adventure movies show the hero returning home with the prize in a race, not only against the villain, but against time itself. If the clock strikes twelve before Cinderella gets home from the ball, her coach will turn into a pumpkin, and she will be again wearing rags.

Unfortunately, the misfortune that was the primary reason for the quest will continue unabated. If your team takes its time to deepen its exploration and perfect its work, the quest itself can be lost. No one knows the precise balance between the desire for further exploration and the demand to return home, but every quest leader needs to constantly reassess these two competing demands.

When pathfinders become enthralled with their discoveries and lose track of time, they have moved into suspended time. Our ancestors knew well the hazards of suspended time. The theme appears in many legends. Consider one of my favorite Welsh legends: the Assembly of the Wondrous Head:

The Welsh king Bran is mortally wounded in a battle. He instructs seven of his warriors to conduct his body to the White Mount, where his head is to be buried facing the Continent, to mystically protect the Islands from impending invasion. Without this act, Britain will be weakened and may fall under the force of multiple invasions. Time is of the essence.

The grief-stricken warriors set out on their quest for the White Mount with their dying king. On the road, the warriors soon encounter friendly strangers, who invite them to a nearby castle for rest and food. The warriors readily accept and find themselves in a marvelous enchanted castle where they indulge themselves with a day and night of feasting. They all feel much refreshed and even King Bran seems to recover a bit. However, time does strange things in enchanted places, and by the time the warriors depart, seven years have passed in the normal world. They rush to White Mount, and King Bran dies en route. The warriors are much too late to stave off the invaders. Their quest has been undone by lost time.

Quest teams I have worked with faced their own time threats. One team's quest to increase hospital throughput was nearly undone by a competitive team, which had started its work later but presented a proposal for solving the problem first. The quest team was still in the middle of its quest and not ready to report back to leadership. Fortunately, leadership recognized that the second team's work was speculative and untested, while the pathfinders had carefully tested their upcoming recommendations. Management continued to support the pathfinders and allowed them more time to complete their mastery and prepare their recommendations. Had the pathfinders delayed any further in presenting their recommendations, the organization could have gone with the other team and settled for pedestrian improvements.

Another quest team became preoccupied with experiments, forgetting time was flying by. They were like King Bran's warriors, becoming lost in an enchanted world of novelty and exploration. They designed and conducted experiment after experiment to create on-time hospital discharges. They always had one more idea to test, one more experiment to run. It took considerable prodding to move them into the next stage of their journey. Many ideas were never implemented, because they had lost the window of opportunity.

Consider the story of two explorers, Burke and Wills. In 1860, they attempted to become the first Europeans to cross Australia from south to north. They led an expedition with a goal similar to that of Lewis and Clark. Burke and Wills wanted to cross the wilderness interior of Australia so the government could find a route for a north-south telegraph line that would eventually bring the country together. Their associate, William Brahe, waited at a temporary base camp with fresh supplies for the remainder of their return trip.

The expedition made it to the mouth of Flinders River, just short of the north coast. Bogged down in mud and running short of supplies, they had to turn back. They finally stumbled into camp, nearly starved, only to discover that Brahe, who had waited for many weeks past their expected return date, folded camp and left only the day before. They struck out after Brahe, who was only hours ahead, but eventually gave up and wandered back to camp. Sadly, Burke and Wills and all but one of their companions perished. They had nearly succeeded in accomplishing their journey. Ultimately, though, they failed, because time had run ahead of them.

Stay Relevant to Organization

It is nearly impossible to manage a pathfinding quest with weekly deadlines. But as a leader, you must keep track of time and the need to progress to the next phase. Watch out for a loss of time urgency. If it happens, remind the team of the probability that they will no longer be relevant if they fail to return results on time. Graph your team's progress against time, but do not set arbitrary interim goals. Many teams find time charts useful when keeping track of time.

Treat suspensions of time as a crisis. If members of your team are temporarily reassigned or the team's work is put on hold, or the team becomes waylaid, your entire quest is threatened. If your team suspends the race, or if you find yourselves in suspended time, the quest is in peril. A leader's job is to sound the alarm if time is suspended.

When pathfinders linger on the quest and slip behind, they run many risks:

- Loss of relevancy back home
- Exposure to unnecessary risks
- Depletion of team resources (people, materials, access to facilities and technology)
- Loss of support from leadership and peers
- Being overtaken by competitors

Successful quests run, in great part, on momentum. Always strive for progress in your race against time. Remember the idle, rainy winter days at Fort Clatsop, near the mouth of the Columbia River, where the Corps of Discovery suffered terribly from inactivity and boredom. Do not allow yourself or the team to be delayed or distracted.

When the quest party presses forward, understanding that time is of the essence, good things happen. There is movement toward wholeness and integration; things come together:

- The team has more time to deal with unexpected obstacles and ride out storms.
- The team has time to exploit short-lived windows of opportunity.
- Team members develop strength and confidence along the way.
- The team's resources and support last through the journey.

Occasionally, organizational pathfinders fight time. They hold back, always keeping their options open to abandon the quest and return to home base. They waste time with their caution and hesitation. Let the team know that there is now no turning back; the only way is through.

Lastly, quests with time urgency do better gaining and maintaining top-level support. Many executives' first reaction to the idea of a quest, or journey into uncharted territory, goes something like this: "That's just what we need. They'll just wander around forever looking for a breakthrough. We don't have time for this!" Don't let the quest become a synonym for wandering without direction. Clearly characterize the quest as a race against time where the precise path is unknown but the goal is clear. That will help you gain and maintain top-level support.

Questions on the Quest

1. What is the nature of the time pressure on your quest?
2. How have you experienced the concept of suspended time?
3. How can you make the race against time meaningful to your fellow pathfinders?

Section Four: Renewal

With the fourth and final phase, Renewal, it is now time to mark your return to home base, to share your breakthrough with the organization. You may need to spread your discovery beyond the scope of the trials your team performed in the previous two phases. You will need an adoption strategy and an implementation plan. During this phase, you will also need to make your final effort to build constituency for adoption of the change. Even the best discovery can fail in implementation if it lacks support. It is time to release control of your discovery so the renewal can spread and begin healing what was broken in the organization. Now is the time to enjoy the fruits of the discovery and use the new capability to create new prosperity. It is also time for you and your pathfinding team to find your new place in the organization.

Sharing the Breakthrough

Renewal literally means taking the organization "back to a state of newness," away from a drift toward stagnation and decline. Sharing the breakthrough (which I have also referred to throughout this book as the prize or great discovery) relieves the underlying state of misfortune and restores the organization to vitality. If you and your team are successful in sharing the breakthrough, the rejuvenating power of the quest will be realized.

As has happened when you passed other milestones, you and your team will face challenges when sharing your prize and when spreading the breakthrough within the organization. This process of adoption can be as simple as declaring that the field trial will now be the new way of working or as difficult as adapting a big change to the needs of many different groups.

Once you have successfully shared the breakthrough, the organization can enjoy a renewed vitality. Your team has not merely restored the organization to past capability; you have helped the organization break through to a higher order of functioning and to a new universe of possibilities.

Transformation

In a successful quest, the organization will experience a rapid advance in knowledge and capability. It can operate at a higher level and pursue opportunities that were unavailable before. In pursuing those opportunities, the organization creates new prosperity.

This milestone marks a time for exploitation of the breakthrough and performing at a higher level of capability. It is a time to exercise new freedom. The transformation creates a platform to pursue higher goals and aspirations. As a result, the organization takes its well-earned place on a bigger playing field.

The quest transforms your team of pathfinders, as well. You have developed new capabilities, tested your leadership skills, and fully engaged in a difficult journey. Upon sharing the gift and sharing the breakthrough, you are ready to take your place at a new level. It is also a well-earned time for reflection. You will expect to ascend in the organization to a position that allows you to put your new confidence and capability to good use. Once exposed to the quest, you and your pathfinders will want to remain engaged in discovery.

There is still much to do to improve performance and create equilibrium within the higher order, but that is work of the business-as-usual organization and not of the quest. Once a cycle of the quest is complete, relative stability will follow. But eventually the seeds of misfortune are sown in another arena. The status quo will be broken, and leaders will once again need to choose between seeking safety and engaging in a new quest. The spiral cycle of renewal, with a new quest — or decline, with the organization's denial of a quest — will begin again.

17. Sharing the Breakthrough

For an occurrence to become an adventure, it is necessary and sufficient for one to recount it.

— Jean-Paul Sartre, 20th c. French philosopher

A few miles downstream from the junction of the Missouri and Yellowstone rivers, the Corps reunites after having split up for a daring return trip. Two days later, Lewis and Clark lead their team back to the Mandan village, where they say goodbye to Charbonneau and Sacagawea, then race for home.

On September 20, 1806, the men notice a cow grazing beside the river and let out a cheer, having reached the first signs of their everyday world. Three days later, after having been gone two and a half years, the Corps finally reaches St. Louis. Residents are amazed to see them, having given them up for dead. The pathfinders are greeted by the city as returning heroes. Lewis writes to President Jefferson that

177

the Corps has arrived safely and that they have "penetrated the Continent of North America to the Pacific Ocean."

The Corps has crossed back over the threshold of adventure, leaving the territory of adventure behind. They now bear the fruit of their quest, the prize of knowledge — contained in the maps, sketches and journals that show their route to the Pacific Ocean — that will transform the United States. Once the prize is shared with those back home, it can start to renew the vitality of the country.

The two captains soon meet with Jefferson in the nation's capital. Undoubtedly, they read excerpts from their journals and show Jefferson a number of maps, sketches, and natural objects from the western side of the continent. It must have been quite a reunion and debriefing session. One wonders if any of them can possibly imagine the long-term legacy of their quest, with Jefferson as sponsor and Lewis and Clark as pathfinding co-leaders.

Know the Prize won't be Welcomed Everywhere

When your pathfinding team returns from its quest, you will carry with you a prize that can create new vitality and prosperity for your organization. You may long for that heroes' welcome. Realize, however, that a period of adjustment is in order before your organization can accept the prize as a potential for renewal. Not everyone may welcome the prize. People in your organization will be forced to decide whether to shift long-held opinions and modes of operation. The moment of truth is here. Will your breakthrough spread within the organization?

If you fail to gain momentum back home, your quest will be diminished. If that happens, the prize will still be of value, but only to your team, which understands its significance. As pathfinders, you are champions of a new way. You need to return, not to be awarded with gold medals, but to serve the organization and work for renewal. You will need to demonstrate the value of the prize, create constituency in support of adoption, and demonstrate flexibility to adapt your gift to home-base conditions.

In many cases, spreading the value of the prize is uncomplicated. Often, by simply maintaining the field trials, the new way becomes standard practice. In other cases, it is a straightforward matter of replicating the field trial into additional areas of the organization.

> Striving for an uncomplicated sharing of the prize is often a great strategy. In one case, a loan department experimented with a flow-based approach to process home loans. Once the field trials were successful, the department simply had to document the new process and work it into their daily operations. In another case, a nursing unit created a new approach to discharging patients. They needed to demonstrate their process for other nurse managers, who took the new methods — with minor modifications — to their units.

Many things can complicate the adoption of the breakthroughs gained through your quest. Your beliefs and values have likely changed as a result of your journey of discovery. Now they may be inconsistent with core beliefs and values of your organization. After a pathfinding team returns from its quest, a manager who was proud of "hunting down and taking out" employees who made significant errors might now be confronted with the demand for a just culture. Both methods perhaps raised standards of quality in the corporation, but the second method proves to be a win-win-win situation for customers, employees, and the organization.

Culture change will not be easy. After undergoing a paradigm shift on your quest, you and your team may be asking different questions than the mainstream organization. A hospital corporation was considering how to reach financial break-even in the emergency room, but the pathfinders were asking a different question: How can we open the emergency-room pipeline so more patients can be admitted quickly and not wait for hours for urgent care? Who cares about emergency-room profit motive if it is strangling the hospital's mission to help people who are suffering (and, as a result, slowing the more profitable admissions to the hospital beds)? The pathfinders' solution for taking care of more patients gave the hospital financial benefits, as well.

On the other hand, there can be difficulties in sharing the prize back home. Once you are changed by the quest, getting back into sync with the organization can present a challenge. Your pathfinding team may simply lack credibility, as measured by standards in the business-as-usual world. If you weren't experts when you started your quest, management wants to know, why should they defer to you now? The answer, of course, is in the results of your field trials, but you must translate those results into business-as-usual terms.

Your Organization May Still Be Adverse to Risk

You will also face typical barriers to large-scale transformation. Even though you have lived with risk every moment of your quest, others in the organization may still be strongly adverse to risk. In one quest, even after the pathfinding team demonstrated the huge productivity gain by putting nurse practitioners in a new role, hospital administrators considered the hiring of more nurse practitioners to be a risky venture and delayed adoption of the idea.

Others have a big stake in maintaining the old way. In another example, a physicians' group had been using an incentive plan based on efficiency. The group had trouble making the shift to a throughput-based workplace. Reducing wait times for patients required that physicians be idle occasionally, undermining their incentive pay system.

Adopting your breakthrough may violate organization structure and traditional turf boundaries. What if, after quest practices are put in place in a hospital, a scrub nurse can now override the wishes of the surgeon if the nurse is not satisfied that all safety requirements have been met? Renewing vitality is transformational and faces classical obstacles to change.

Plan Adoption of the Breakthrough

A common barrier to adoption is scalability. Your pathfinding team has run field trials of the prize during the discovery and mastery phases of your journey, but adoption of the prize on an organizational scale can be much greater in scope. This demands careful planning of target adopters, sequencing, resources, adaptation, communication, training and so on. Spreading the breakthrough on this scale may require project charters, project plans, implementation teams, project managers, budgets and metrics. Pathfinders may work with the adoption on only the first one or two sites, letting others do much of the implementation work. When scalability is an issue, project management approaches now make a lot of sense.

After the long wilderness adventure, Lewis was overcome with trouble adjusting to his new life in the everyday world. It took his steady co-leader, Clark, to orchestrate and publish the journals that were vital to sharing the quest with the country. Your pathfinding team may need to make careful plans to spread the benefits of your quest.

Tell the Truth about the Breakthrough

Like a physician who cannot force her patients to take their medicine, you cannot force the organization to benefit from your discovery. All you can do is offer it with humility. Like all responsibilities on the quest, your offer of the discovery demands much. It demands that you be a truth teller. How well does the breakthrough really work? What does it require of the user?

The quest demands that you find the courage to make a case for adoption, even in the face of skepticism and stiff resistance back at home base. It asks you to reach out to everyone and engage them in the new concept, allowing them to make it their own. You will need tenacity to complete this last phase of the quest, even if others seem ambivalent about the costs of renewal. If you meet the demands of this final phase, you have succeeded. In a sense, you have journeyed to the ocean and returned to publish your precious maps and journals. Let go. The rest is up to the organization.

Questions for the Quest

Now that you are back at home base, consider drawing some conclusions about your quest:

1. *Your story.* What is the story of your quest? How will you tell it? How can others become part of your story? How can everyone hear it?

2. *Your role in adoption.* Will you take an active role in the spread of your breakthrough, or will you pass the new way to a project implementation team?

3. *Your role as an expert.* Will you be the expert source on the breakthrough? Will you develop new practices?

4. *Target adopters.* Who should adopt first? Who are the most likely to be willing to adopt early? Who is most likely to succeed?

5. *Your role as a constituency builder.* Will you be responsible for building support for adopting the breakthrough?

6. *Demonstration and communication.* In what ways will you communicate the breakthrough to the organization and to your audience? How can you show, rather than just talk about, the quest?

7. *Customization.* Will you urge adopters to adopt without revision, or do you want them to adapt your breakthrough to their circumstances? Less adaptation could mean more resistance, but too much adaptation may result in dilution of the value of the breakthrough.

8. *Spread tactics.* Do you want to share the prize quickly or gradually? Will adoption of the prize be voluntary or mandated?

9. *Monitoring.* How will you monitor the spread? What measures will be useful?

10. *Project management.* Would the spread activities benefit from project management? How would project management be helpful if you plan to replicate the adoption in several areas?

18. Transformation
17. Sharing the Breakthrough

18. Transformation

The highest reward for a person's toil is not what they get for it, but what they become by it.
— John Ruskin, English author and social critic

In late September 1806, Lewis and Clark and the Corps of Discovery arrive in St. Louis and are received as heroes. With them they bring the gift of new knowledge about the West that will electrify the country and soon fuel westward expansion.

Some say that Lewis and Clark fell short of the goals of their quest. After all, they found that accounts of a Northwest Passage, an almost unbroken navigable path between the headwaters of the Mississippi and the rivers flowing into the Pacific Ocean, were only folklore. Undoubtedly, Jefferson is disappointed on this point, but the Northwest Passage was never Jefferson's primary motivation for the Expedition.

Jefferson needs a story about a future America, a young nation that spanned the continent. His greater objective is a new identity for Americans: they will be seen by the world as powerful people with unlimited opportunities and resources and room for ever-growing potential. Lewis and Clark give him that: an epic story that changes the dreams and destiny of America.

America will be transformed not only by the story of the expedition, but also by Lewis and Clarks' geographical breakthrough. Boats will never sail a Northwest Passage, but the telegraph lines and railroads will follow in Lewis and Clarks' footsteps and unite the fledgling country. New American immigrants will soon move into Lewis and Clarks' map, spreading from the Eastern seaboard across the entire continent. America has transformed itself from an outpost on the Atlantic into a transcontinental power, a country to be reckoned with. The Lewis and Clark Expedition is a change in state for America.

As with many transformations, there are also tragic consequences of the Expedition. Subsequent expansion of European Americans obliterates many Native Americans peoples and cultures. Native American populations decline from epidemic diseases brought from the East, violence at the hands of explorers and colonists, destruction of their food sources, and displacement from their lands.

Help Your Organization Transform

As your organization adopts and spreads the breakthrough, it will begin to transform and renew itself. Others will even use their creatively to extend the use of the breakthrough into new areas not considered by your pathfinding team. Early adopters will identify and solve a number of problems, quickly making full use of the new discovery.

As the new way comes into general practice, the organization will achieve a change to a higher level of capability. The emergency department mentioned in the previous chapters did not only operate more efficiently; it operated with a higher order capability and achieved results that would have been impossible in its previous state, regardless of the resources expended. Yet it achieved breakthrough results in this new state with the same level of resources. The emergency department was now operating with stability at the new level. That is how transformation should work at the culmination of your quest.

With the step-change in capability comes the ability to exploit that capability for the benefit of customers, employees, and suppliers. That, in turn, creates the opportunity for financial rewards. In *Evolution: The General Theory*, Ervin Laszlo argues that higher-order systems are simpler than lower-order ones and can control many of the lower-order systems that previously had to be controlled separately. The combination of simplicity and control over lower-order functions means a step-change in performance and lower operating costs.

Breakthroughs don't push existing systems harder. They create higher-order systems that supercharge the lower-level systems. For example, an insurance company did not attempt to fix problems in the existing system. Instead, it radically changed the whole experience for the insurance agent. The lower-order systems were still trying to process applications, underwrite policies, and pay agents. But the new, higher-order system organized the functions around a rapid and hassle-free agent experience. In this way, organizations break through to a new state characterized by a step-change in performance.

The technical part of the transformation is complete. Further changes in the organization's culture and the practice of leadership will follow. Eventually, a period of what is called dynamic stability will follow. This is the time when the organization can exploit, perfect, and extend their new capability. The organization has renewed its capacity to create value and benefit. It will extend the corporate life cycle and postpone stagnation and decline long enough to launch a future quest. If all has gone well, the quest is complete, and the organization — with respect to the call to adventure — is renewed. The Quest Effect has worked.

The next quest will take place in a different domain, but the basic archetypal pattern and features will not vary. The underlying structure of the quest remains the same from one Call to Adventure to the next. New quests will continue to emerge. That is the cycle of renewal.

Experience Personal Transformation and Renewal

Individuals as well as organizations are transformed by the quest. Pathfinders, upon their conclusion of the quest, are different people than those who embarked. In the epic of Lewis and Clark, it is now time for the members of the Corps of Discovery to be acclaimed and take their new place in society.

The captains travel to Washington D.C. and are honored with balls and galas as they pass through towns. The men of the Corps are awarded double pay and given 320 acres of land for their achievement, while Lewis and Clark each receive 1,600 acres of land. Jefferson appoints Lewis governor of the Lower Louisiana Territory. Clark is made the Indian agent for the West and brigadier general of the upper Louisiana Territory's militia. As is true for most successful quests, the rewards are great.

Sadly, Lewis' tragic fate underscores the extraordinary difficulty some experience in adjusting to everyday life after a peak experience such as the expedition. He stays in Philadelphia to arrange for publication of the all-important journals, eventually arriving in the South a year late to assume his position as governor. Unsuited for the demands, he makes a poor governor and sinks into depression. After living the peak experience of the expedition, the life of a politician must have felt extremely confining to a man like Lewis. The mysterious circumstances surrounding his death, which most historians agree was a suicide, so soon after the celebration of the expedition's success, have been a topic of conversation for the past two hundred years.

The fate of the men of the Corps is a mixed bag. About one third of the men return to the territory they had crossed with the Corps, becoming trappers and traders. Another third settles on the wilderness frontier in Missouri, Illinois, and Indiana. Some, like Sergeant Patrick Gass, who lived to the age of 93, are able to see the fruit of their quest through the decades. Others are not so fortunate. Clark's slave, York, is understandably furious that Clark decides not to give him his promised freedom after York's valued work on the expedition. It takes almost ten years before Clark frees him. Sacagawea dies of an unknown illness in 1812 at a South Dakota army outpost; she is only about 24 years old.

After Lewis's death, Clark is the one who makes sure the journals are published. Philadelphia editor Nicholas Biddle edits the journals and, in 1814, publishes the History of the Expedition under the Command of Captains Lewis and Clark.

For each of the Corps members, the Lewis and Clark Expedition was the turning point of their lives. Lives that experienced such dramatic transformation are not easily put back on an ordinary track. It can be a huge challenge to re-engage with the everyday world after the emotional highs and great gains of a quest.

Carve Out a New Place

Once you and your pathfinding team have brought home the prize – the breakthrough that can bring healing and recovery — turn your attention to taking your place in the organization and helping your companions do the same. It is easy, in the glow of the acclaim, to assume that others will act in the same way they did before you undertook your quest. Releasing control of your career to others after an exhausting quest may even seem appealing. However, without your attention and personal steps, you could easily find yourself in the wasteland of perpetually longing for a new peak experience.

Like the seasoned soldiers who returned home with Lewis and Clark, organizational pathfinders return in a different state than when they departed. Even though the quest itself was probably exhausting, many return with new energy and a readiness to play on a larger stage. Their success and sense of completion brings about new confidence. Their experiences provide them with new capabilities. They are ready to perform on a higher level.

Even if your pathfinding team returns triumphant from your quest, there are no guarantees about what comes next. Much depends on your pathfinding team's understanding of the situation and the freedom to apply new capabilities. Success after the quest also depends on the organization's ability to carve out a new place for the returning heroes. Although they will return the same people who started the quest, they will not be able to simply return to old roles.

A pathfinder named Connie guided one quest that created a breakthrough in emergency healthcare services. As a result, the hospital corporation won loyal customers, as well as a great deal of positive publicity. The corporation built a financial turnaround by adopting the breakthrough that Connie's team discovered and mastered. Connie received industry awards and recognition, but her own manager refused to pay her an expected bonus, because she missed one rather trivial operational goal. It was clear to Connie that she would not find her place after the quest within her organization. She left several months later and found rewarding work helping other hospitals apply the breakthroughs she helped pioneer. By withholding much-deserved rewards from Connie, the corporation lost a capable leader and spawned new competitors in emergency care.

Another healthcare leader was not fully recognized for her leadership in a quest that transformed a hospital's surgery center. When she returned to managing surgical services, she felt no longer stimulated in her old job. She left to head up the operation of a new ambulatory surgical center. The new challenges used the capabilities she had developed on the earlier quest. One of the surgeons reported that she was essential in designing the new surgical operations.

Create a Platform for Higher Goals

It is the responsibility of you and your fellow pathfinders to accept the benefits of the quest. It is no time to shy away from awards and acclaim. Recognition creates a platform from which pathfinders can leverage their new capabilities and experiences. Recognition and acclaim have short lives, so they cannot be deferred until some later time. Use this welcoming home to your advantage. It can give you the freedom to create a new place for yourself and your companions after the quest.

Use your homecoming as a grace period for redemption. You can win back reputation, make good on old promises, and extricate yourself from confining obligations. If your career was stalling, this is the time for resurgence and fresh opportunities. If there are old wounds, this may be the time for healing. Use this opportunity to reestablish yourself as an innovator, and assume a new level; your hard-won capabilities can add value to your organization.

Occasionally the financial rewards are substantial enough that you will enjoy a new personal prosperity. Expect rewards at the conclusion of the quest. You have earned them, and they can give you the freedom to do great things in the future. In any case, do not allow yourself to be returned to your old position and previous pay with a simple token of appreciation. Know that you are now more valuable to your organization and others.

Fall down Six Times, Get up Seven

What if your team's quest failed? As Pulitzer-Prize-winning biologist Edward O. Wilson said, "If those committed to the quest fail, they will be forgiven. When lost, they will find another way." The pathfinders will still be acclaimed and be asked to take a new place in the organization, provided, in Wilson's words, "the effort is honorable and failure memorable."

As the old saying goes, "Fall down six times; get up seven." pathfinders who refuse to accept the role of victim, even in failure, will be honored for their courage to overcome their situation. Ernest Shackleton, possibly the greatest hero of the Age of Exploration, completely failed to achieve his quest to cross Antarctica. Yet he was able to bring his entire crew home safely after battling the most arduous conditions imaginable. Make sure the organization hears how you fought for success and how you and your companions grew as a result.

Use Your New Capability for Good

While pathfinders develop new capabilities on the quest, they can also return with new issues. Sometimes their confidence, when combined with new acclaim, can turn into conceit and arrogance. Others will resist adopting the breakthroughs because of the insufferable boasting of a returning pathfinder. When your team is aware of this tendency, members can harness their sense of pride in accomplishment.

Returning pathfinders often have new allies and new enemies. People gain and lose when new changes are adopted, and some will seek to block or undermine the pathfinders after their return. Work on building constituency for adoption of the prize you fought so hard to find. If you are a manager or executive, help your team gain support.

You and your pathfinders can feel like strangers in your own organization when you return from your quest. Their capabilities and values may have changed drastically. I worked with a group of information technology professionals in the healthcare field who were investigating the principles of High Reliability Organizations (HROs). By talking with experts in HRO, the pathfinders discovered how to adapt those principles to their own organization.

Their question was, "How can we significantly reduce the potential for hazard and harm to our patients?" Returning from their quest, these pathfinders were simply unwilling to return to their business-as-usual lives. Once the members saw the potential of their new discovery in clinical as well as IT areas, they were committed to change the way the whole organization treated patients. Two of those involved dedicated their energies to transforming the clinical side of their organization into a full-fledged HRO.

After the quest, the business-as-usual world can be decidedly un-stimulating. After the peak experiences associated with the quest, everyday work easily becomes dull and even depressing. Pathfinders disengage.

If you find yourself disengaging, remember the examples of Lewis and Clark. Clark found ways to use his newfound capabilities, while Lewis did not and sank into depression. Ask yourself if you are effectively using the capabilities that you developed on the quest; if not, change your work. Do not allow yourself to adapt to diminishment after working at a peak level.

Corporations are smart if they work hard to retain pathfinders. These pathfinders exhibit the very qualities that my clients in top organizations often say are in short supply. Returning pathfinders are motivated. They are accustomed to leading and contributing. They refuse to be victims, and they routinely overcome obstacles. They collaborate and are innovative. They are stimulated by novelty and interested in change.

Most of all, they have experienced the joy of finding a great discovery and creating something of value – and they want more. They will dedicate themselves to a future act of creation. Part of the prize they bring back is a more capable version of themselves.

The following are some personal steps that can help you take your place after the quest:

- *Allow time to recover.* Quests are exhausting; you cannot operate at full potential immediately after a quest. Take some time to relax and refresh yourself. This would be a great time for some vacation. New meaning will emerge when you are rested.

- *Re-chart your future.* Consider how the quest changes what you can accomplish in the future. Recalibrate your goals and objectives. Never adapt to the diminishment of obsolete roles. Think about what it will take to keep you stimulated and engaged. Mike directed the terminal operations of a major international airport. He was also part of a pathfinder team that took the airport to world-class levels of customer service. After participating in a quest, he reset his aspirations for leadership. Within a year, he stepped up to be CEO of another major airport.

- *Consolidate your new capabilities.* Take inventory of what you learned on the quest. What can you do now that you could not do at the outset? How has your outlook changed? Think about how you now solve problems and innovate. You may have had new experiences leading others. You may be skilled in using new tools and methods. You may know more than anyone about the new breakthrough and how to harness it. So figure out what you can do, what you want to do, and how you can package your capabilities for the next level of engagement. Stella set out on a quest to learn to play the Celtic harp and provide therapeutic music at the bedside of patients. She recorded two music CDs and wrote a book for other musicians who also wanted to play music at the bedside. When she consolidated her new capabilities, she realized that she could engage musicians everywhere. She eventually became the director of an organization that certifies musicians to play at the bedside.

- *Find another quest.* Quests revitalize organizations, yet there are dramatically too few quests. As a result, organizations

195

and those in them suffer. Is there another adventure calling you? Consider proposing a new venture to create another breakthrough. I met Tom, a surgeon, on a team when we were working to increase throughput of surgical cases. He contributed to several breakthrough innovations. One source of wasted time was looking for lost surgical sponges, which were sometimes found in the patient. Later, when our project was completed, we started another quest to instantly detect sponges retained in patients after surgery.

- *Help others quest.* In addition to leading a quest, you can encourage others to initiate their own journeys. You have been on an organizational quest, and you know what to expect. Others can use your wisdom and encouragement. Find those who are sounding their call to adventure, and offer your help. It may be your turn to be the guide. Remember, someone helped you launch your quest.

- *Sponsor a quest.* One way to help others is to sponsor a quest, just as President Jefferson sponsored the Lewis and Clark Expedition. Jim, an insurance industry manager, won a major leadership award and the highest possible evaluation after completing his quest to turn around his division. After he was promoted to another division, he sponsored a quest to reshape customer relationships. He inspired others to lead large parts of the new effort.

Questions for the Quest

1. How will you re-engage with the everyday world when you return from your quest?

2. How can you make a satisfying place for yourself and your fellow pathfinders within your organization or industry?
3. If your quest is not deemed a success, how will you and your companions handle the situation?
4. Where are the new opportunities to quest again?

Epilogue: The Never Ending Quest

If you want to succeed you should strike out on new paths, rather than travel the worn paths of accepted success.
— John D. Rockefeller, American industrialist and philanthropist

On September 23, 1806, Lewis and Clark spend their last day as members of the Corps of Discovery. They had been gone for two and a half years and been given up for dead by most Americans. Even though their return was long overdue and they failed to find the fabled Northwest Passage, their journey succeeded beyond all measures. It is a breakthrough for America. Their legacy will be vast.

Lewis and Clark's great breakthrough opens the West to Americans, but the change emerges slowly. During the following thirty-five years, little changes until, in 1841 and 1842, the first wagon trains leave for the West Coast. The great westward expansion progresses at a relatively slow pace, extending over several decades.

However, that period of gradual change does not last. As Americans settles the West, a new call to adventure is sounded. Visionaries call on the American government to re-unite the citizens of the United States, now dispersed across a vast continent. Throughout the 1850s, they petition Congress for funds to create a transcontinental telegraph system to tie dispersed Americans together. At last, in 1861 Western Union complete the first transcontinental telegraph. Americans communicate from coast to coast at nearly instantaneous speeds. Just eight years later, the last spike is driven for the first transcontinental railroad. Transcontinental communication and travel that took years in Lewis and Clark's Expedition can be accomplished in mere minutes or days. The quest to create the transcontinental telegraph suddenly and radically changes the world — again.

Ensure that the Quest Is Never Ending

Lewis and Clark's adventure was one cycle in a never-ending spiral of quests, each quest breaking through to a new level. Each quest was followed by a period of relative stability. Each period of stability was interrupted by a new quest.

By successfully completing its quest, organizations will make the leap to a new level of capability and prosperity that was previously beyond its grasp. They will likely enjoy a stable interlude of continuous growth and refinement as they exploit recent breakthroughs. Pathfinders will be influential and respected. These are the bounties of the quest.

What was unexplored territory a short time ago will become part of the new home base — the new norm. The quest itself will pass into memory — becoming a version of the story about a "bright and shining moment" when the organization broke free of its normal constraints. As stability returns, the new way will become standard work, roles will be defined, facilities completed, performance expectations recalibrated, and improvement methods put in place. The home-base structures that create stability and equilibrium will reassert themselves to protect and exploit newfound gains.

The interlude of stability may last for decades or may be all too short. Eventually, each stable plateau will be interrupted by a new interval of quest, a new opportunity for breakthrough. This is vital, since organizations can only renew themselves when periods of stable plateaus are interspersed with breakthrough intervals, setting up leaps to ever-more ambitious levels.

This is the never-ending quest – a spiral of ever-more-ambitious cycles of development, each revitalizing the organization. Of course, some quests will fail, but failure is simply part of the development process, creating opportunities for new quests. However, denying the need to quest, and thereby stopping the cycle altogether, is fatal. After a few cycles of lost opportunities or disregarded threats, the organization will no longer be able to recover. Doggedly pursuing safety, or the perception of safety, while obstructing the quest is a terminal behavior. Without the quest, the organization will die, be acquired, or languish indefinitely in a withered state.

After completing your quest, you have two fundamental leadership responsibilities:

1. Help exploit the newfound capabilities for the benefit and renewal of your organization (and beyond).
2. More importantly, ensure that the cycle of renewal continues. Do not allow exploitation to squeeze out exploration. Ensure that your organization's potential to quest is never-ending.

Make the Quest Personal

D.M. Dooling, former editor of *Parabola*, wrote, "How terrible to think of not being the hero of one's own life." She goes on: "And if the part seems too big, if we picture the hero as being 'more than life-sized,' it is because our daily life has dwindled, become less than real, and only small proportions seem natural to us...."

Do not settle for only small proportions. The quests you have experienced are the way life is meant to be lived. Take your new place with humility, and set your sights high for the next quest in your life's journey. As Gandhi said, "Our life is a long and arduous quest after Truth." Your quest within an organization is just one chapter.

Perhaps physician and microbiologist Charles Pasternak said it best: "It is in man's very nature to seek, not just for basic needs or personal comfort, but also beyond his own requirements or those of his generation, to climb mountains because they are there, to study and experiment for the sake of knowledge, and to voyage to the moon and beyond."

Take your rightful place, and be ready. Your next quest may be just around the corner.

Paths cannot be taught; they can only be taken.

— *Zen saying*

Please visit QuestEffect.com for additional information and materials that support this book.

Selected References

1. Ichak Adizes. 1988. Corporate lifecycles: How and Why Corporations Grow and Die and What to Do About It. Englewood Cliffs, N.J: Prentice Hall

2. Rebecca Chan Allen. 2002. Guiding Change Journeys: a Synergistic Approach to Organization Transformation. San Francisco: Jossey-Bass/Pfeiffer,

3. Stephen E. Ambrose. 1996. Undaunted courage: Meriwether Lewis, Thomas Jefferson, and the opening of the American West. New York: Simon & Schuster

4. Karen Armstrong. 2006. A Short History of Myth. Canongate U.S.

5. Michael Beer. 2000. Breaking the Code of Change. Harvard Business School Press

6. James Bonnet. 2006. Stealing Fire from the Gods. Studio City, CA: Michael Wiese Productions

7. William Bridges. 1991. Managing Transitions: Making the Most of Change. Reading, Mass: Addison-Wesley

8. Moyra Caldecott. 1996. Mythical Journeys, Legendary Quests. London: Blandford

9. Joseph Campbell. 1968. The Hero with a Thousand Faces. New Jersey: Princeton University Press

10. Joseph Campbell with Bill Moyers. 1988. The Power of Myth. New York: Doubleday

11. Clayton M. Christensen. 1997. The Innovator's Dilemma: The Revolutionary Book that Will Change the Way You Do Business. New York: HarperBusiness

12. Clayton M. Christensen, Michael E. Raynor. 2003. The Innovator's Solution: Creating and Sustaining Successful Growth. Harvard Business School Press

13. Roger Connors, Tom Smith, Craig Hickman. 1994. The Oz Principle: Getting Results through Individual and Organizational Accountability. Englewood Cliffs: Prentice Hall

14. Roger Connors, Tom Smith. 1999. Journey to the Emerald City: Achieve A Competitive Edge by Creating A Culture of Accountability. Paramus, NJ: Prentice Hall Press

15. D. M. Dooling. 1994. The Spirit of Quest. Morning Light Press

16. Sandy Dunlop. 2001. Business Heroes: Making Business Renewal You Personal Crusade. John Wiley & Sons

17. Viktor E. Frankl. 1992. Man's Search for Meaning: An Introduction to Logotherapy. Boston: Beacon Press

18. Sarah W. Fraser. 2004. Accelerating the Spread of Good Practice: A Workbook for Health Care. Kingsham Press Ltd

19. Edwin Friedman. 2007. A Failure of Nerve: Leadership in the Age of the Quick Fix. Seabury Books

20. Laurence Gonzales. 2004. Deep Survival: Who Lives, Who Dies, and Why: True Stories of Miraculous Endurance and Sudden Death. New York: W.W. Norton & Co

21. Robert A. Johnson. 1991. Transformation. San Francisco: HarperSanFrancisco

22. The Journals of Lewis and Clark. 1997. Boston: Houghton Mifflin Co

23. C. G. Jung. 1968. The Archetypes and the Collective Unconscious. Princeton: Princeton University Press

24. Rosalind Kerven. 1996. The Mythical Quest. Pomegranate

25. John P. Kotter. 1996. Leading Change. Boston: Harvard Business School Press

26. Alfred Lansing. 1999. Endurance: Shackleton's Incredible Voyage. Carroll & Graf Publishers

27. Ervin Laszlo. 1996. Evolution: The General Theory: Advances in Systems Theory, Complexity & the Human Sciences. Cresskill, NJ: Hampton Press

28. Thomas Malory. 1986. Le Morte d'Arthur. Scribner Paper Fiction

29. Margaret Mark and Carol S. Pearson. 2001. The Hero and the Outlaw: Building Extraordinary Brands through the Power of Archetypes. New York: McGraw-Hill

30. John Matthews. 1991. The Grail. New York: Thames and Hudson

31. Gary McAuley. 2001. The Hero's Journey. Sunwest

32. Larry E. Morris. 2004. The Fate of the Corps: What Became of the Lewis and Clark Explorers After the Expedition. New Haven: Yale University Press

33. Richard E. Nisbett. 2003. The Geography of Thought. New York: Free Press

34. Harrison Owen. 1987. Spirit. Potomac, MD: Abbott Publishing

35. Harrison Owen. 1991. Riding the Tiger: Doing Business in a Transforming World. Potomac, MD: Abbott Publishing

36. Harrison Owen. 1999. The Spirit of Leadership: Liberating the Leader in Each of Us. Berrett-Koehler Publishers

37. Charles Pasternak. 2003. Quest: The Essence of Humanity. Chichester: Wiley

38. Carol S. Pearson. 1991. Awakening the Heroes Within: Twelve Archetypes to Help us Find ourselves and Transform our World. San Francisco: HarperSanFrancisco

39. Carol S. Pearson. 1998. The Hero Within: Six Archetypes We Live By. San Francisco: HarperSanFrancisco

40. Jordan B. Peterson. 1999. Maps of Meaning. New York: Routledge
41. Robert E. Quinn. 1996. Deep change: Discovering the Leader Within. San Francisco: Jossey-Bass Publishers
42. Otto Rank, Lord Fitzroy Richard Somerset Raglan and Alan Dundes. 1990. In Quest of the Hero. Princeton, N.J: Princeton University Press
43. Paul Rebillot, Melissa Kay. 1993. The Call to Adventure. San Francisco: HarperSanFrancisco
44. Everett M. Rogers. 1995. Diffusion of Innovations. New York: Free Press
45. Jeff Salz. 2000. The Way of Adventure. New York: Wiley
46. Tony Smith. 1993. Parzival's Briefcase: Six Practices and New Philosophy for Healthy Organizational Change. San Francisco: Chronicle Books
47. David Spangler. 1996. The Call. Riverhead Hardcover
48. Ralph D. Stacey. 1992. Managing the Unknowable: Strategic Boundaries Between Order and Chaos in Organizations. Jossey-Bass
49. Christopher Vogler. 1982. The writer's journey. Studio City, CA: M. Wiese Productions
50. Marie-Louise Von Franz. 1997. Archetypal Dimensions of the Psyche. Shambhala
51. Margaret J. Wheatley. 1992. Leadership and the New Science: Discovering Order in a Chaotic World. San Francisco: Berrett-Koehler Publishers
52. David Whyte. 1996. The Heart Aroused: Poetry and the Preservation of the Soul in Corporate America. Currency
53. David Whyte. 2001. Crossing the Unknown Sea: Work as a Pilgrimage of Identity. Riverhead Hardcover

54. Aaron Wildavsky. 1988. Searching for Safety. New Brunswick: Transaction Books
55. Larry Wilson, Hersch Wilson. 1998. Play to Win! Revised Edition: Getting Results through Individual and Organizational Accountability. Bard Press

Randall Benson is an author, speaker, and business consultant. He earned his MBA in Operations Management from the University of Washington. Since his first high-tech startup over thirty years ago, he has helped organizations achieve breakthrough performance. Formerly North American director for World Class International and senior consultant with Coopers and Lybrand, he also holds U.S. patents on emerging technologies, and his projects have been referenced in over eighty major media spots. A management expert who uses the disciplines of psychology, complexity theory, mythology, history, and evolutionary science to guide individuals and organizations on transformational journeys, his work has been noted in several business books, including *Leadership without Excuses* and *Synchro Service*. He and his wife live in the San Juan Islands in Washington State. Contact him at rbenson@questeffect.com.

Margaret D. Smith has co-authored or edited more than twenty books for clients, ranging from a story about one woman's overcoming of breast cancer (Stealing the Dragon's Fire, by Clo Wilson-Hashiguchi) to a first-person account of a World War II airman (Tales of a Tail Gunner, by Eddie Picardo). A poet and musician, she is the author of six books of her own, including A Holy Struggle: Unspoken Thoughts of Hopkins (WaterBrook), Journal Keeper (Eerdmans), and Barn Swallow (Brass Weight). Contact her at margaret.arts@gmail.com.

5956383R0

Made in the USA
Charleston, SC
26 August 2010